JOHN AND THÉRÈSE: FLAMES OF LOVE

John and Thérèse: Flames of Love

The influence of St. John of the Cross in the Life and Writings of St. Thérèse of Lisieux

GUY GAUCHER
Auxiliary Bishop of Bayeux and Lisieux

Translated by Alexandra Plettenberg-Serban
English editing by Bernadette Frenzel

ST PAULS

Originally published (1996) in French by Les Éditions du Cerf,
29, bd de Latour-Maubourg, 75007 Paris under the title
*Flammes D'Amour: Thérèse et Jean. L'Influence de saint Jean de la Croix
dans la vie et les écrits de sainte Thérèse de Lisieux.*

Library of Congress Cataloging-in-Publication Data

Gaucher, Guy, 1930-
    [Flammes d'amour. English]
    John and Thérèse: flames of love: the influence of St. John of the Cross
in the life and writings of St. Thérèse of Lisieux / Guy Gaucher; translated by
Alexandra Plettenberg-Serban; English editing by Bernadette Frenzel.
        p.   cm.
    Includes bibliographical references.
    ISBN 0-8189-0824-6
    1. Thérèse of Lisieux, Saint, 1873-1997.   2. Christian saints — France —
Lisieux — Biography.   3. Spirituality — Catholic Church — History —
19th century.   4. John of the Cross, Saint, 1542-1591 — Influence.
    I. Title.
BX4700.T5G37513   1999
282'.092—dc21   98-36037
[B]   CIP

Produced and designed in the United States of America by the
Fathers and Brothers of the Society of St. Paul,
2187 Victory Boulevard, Staten Island, New York 10314-6603,
as part of their communications apostolate.

ISBN: 0-8189-0824-6

Printing Information:

Current Printing - first digit   3   4   5   6   7   8   9   10

Year of Current Printing - first year shown

        2006 2007 2008 2009 2010 2011 2012 2013 2014

TABLE OF CONTENTS

INTRODUCTION TO THE ENGLISH VERSION

WHEN BISHOP GUY GAUCHER PUBLISHED THIS book in 1996, he was hoping that it might contribute to the proclamation of St. Thérèse of Lisieux as Doctor of the Church. One year later, on October 19, 1997, the request by the author and more than 300,000 members of the Church who had worked since 1932 for this goal, was finally granted by Pope John Paul II.

In fact, in this extraordinary study Thérèse is presented as a Doctor of Love and as a "truly modern saint," a woman who takes the "fast way," the "way of the elevator" directly into the normally very inaccessible mysticism of St. John of the Cross, one of the greatest mystics of all times. She desires to live by the very core of that mysticism: Love! And to do so in a quite ordinary and little way, one that is accessible to limitless numbers and kinds of people. Her success is due in no small measure to the new and astoundingly free way in which she reads John of the Cross, as well as the New Testament. This points again to her courageously focused and unique independence of thinking and feeling.

Bishop Gaucher, a well-known author and eminent authority on St. Thérèse, meticulously traces John's influence on the young Carmelite nun and finds that he has been a presence that guided and inspired her throughout her short life. No other book about Thérèse's spirituality unfolds so completely what this young saint really meant by "the flames of love." We are thereby able, as it were, to gain entrance into the heart of all her poetry and the meaning of her very life: "To love Jesus and to make him loved." It also seems that, in following her into this essence of her vocation and mission, we are also enabled to have a new — or perhaps, the very first — understanding of the great Spanish saint and mystic.

We wish to express our gratitude to the author, Bishop Guy Gaucher, and to thank Fr. Edmund C. Lane, S.S.P. and the staff at Alba House.

New York, April 19, 1998

TRANSLATOR'S NOTE

To help the reader use this book most efficiently, we would like to indicate the following modifications we have made to the author's references and/or citations:

• We have provided supplementary information to enhance the reader's understanding of historical European characters and circumstances, as well as more detailed citations especially for texts available in English; this is given as bracketed footnotes, to distinguish them from the author's, and/or by (—Trans.).

• We have supplied English titles in brackets for French titles that have not been published in English translation, to clarify the meaning of the reference.

• Supplementary details of English pagination are bracketed within the text or footnotes.

• We have created a new ABBREVIATIONS (using the English publications wherever possible and adding explanatory material) and have incorporated some material from the author's ABBREVIATIONS into the BIBLIOGRAPHY (likewise with additional material for the English version).

• We have used our own translation of Biblical references in order to render the author's given text. They are abbreviated and numbered according to those of The Jerusalem Bible:

2 Co	2 Corinthians	Lk	Luke
Col	Colossians	Mt	Matthew
Dt	Deuteronomy	1 Pet	1 Peter
Ex	Exodus	Ph	Philippians
Heb	Hebrews	Ps	Psalm
Ho	Hosea	Rom	Romans
Is	Isaiah	Rv	Revelation
Jn	John	Sg	Song of Songs

ABBREVIATIONS

- All quotations from St. Thérèse and St. John of the Cross are taken from the ICS translations of the French critical editions of the works of St. Thérèse of Lisieux and St. John of the Cross whenever possible. This method was chosen so that the English reader has direct access to the major references used by the author (cf. Bibliography). The sometimes unusual ICS punctuation follows Thérèse's own distinctive use of exclamation points, emphases, majuscules, suspension points, etc. Unless otherwise noted, the abbreviations and referencing system used in the ICS Publications volumes follow that of the French critical editions. More complete bibliographical information appears at the end of this volume.
- English translations of other works cited by the author are used whenever possible.
- "Mgr." is an abbreviation for "Monseigneur," a French title of honor for members of the Catholic episcopacy; it is thus not a precise equivalent to the word "Monsignor" in American usage. The term "Sisters" is used here to refer to religious women, some of whom in the Lisieux Carmel were also Thérèse's blood "sisters."

Writings of St. Thérèse

Ms A, B, C Thérèse's autobiographical manuscripts, with indication of page numbers (in the ICS Publications edition) and recto or verso side. For example, Ms B, p. 194 (3v°) refers to p. 194 of *Story of a Soul*, the verso side of p. 3 of the second manuscript (B). This referencing system is incorporated into the ICS Publications third edition of SS.

CJ   The "Yellow Notebook" (*Carnet jaune*) of Mother Agnès [Pauline], as found in HLC. The numbers indicate month, day and entry; e.g., CJ 7.27.5 indicates the fifth saying on July 27.

DE   *Derniers entretiens* as found in HLC. The numbers indicate month, day and entry; e.g., DE 8.31.9 indicates the ninth saying on August 31.

GC I & II *General Correspondence*, vol. I and II, followed by the page number.

HLC   *Her Last Conversations*, translated from DE (followed by page numbers in ICS Publications editions).

LT   Thérèse's letters, numbered and paginated according to the critical edition (GC).

PN   Thérèse's poems, numbered according to the critical edition (*Poetry*, sometimes followed by the page number).

Pri   Thérèse's prayers, numbered according to the critical edition (*Prayers*, sometimes followed by the page number).

RP   Thérèse's *Pious Recreations* (i.e., *Plays*), numbered according to the critical edition (NEC or Œ/T).

NEC   *Nouvelle Édition du Centenaire.* (*New Centenary Edition*, in 8 volumes.)

Œ/T   *Œuvres complètes de sainte Thérèse de Lisieux.* (*Collected Works* of St. Thérèse of Lisieux, in one volume.)

Works About St. Thérèse

AL   *Annales de Lisieux.* (Magazine *Annals of Lisieux.*)
BT   *La Bible avec Thérèse de Lisieux.* (*The Bible with Thérèse of Lisieux.*)
CRM   *Carnet Rouge.* (*Red Notebook*, edited by Sr. Marie of the Trinity.)
CSG   Sr. Geneviève's *Conseils et Souvenirs.*
CSM   *Conseils et Souvenirs.* (*Counsels and Reminiscences* edited by Sr. Marie of the Trinity.)
FTL   *Visage de Thérèse de Lisieux*, followed by volume number and numbered photo of Thérèse. (Translated by Peter-Thomas Rohrbach, under the title *The Photo Album of St. Thérèse of Lisieux.*)

MSG   Sr. Geneviève's *A Memoir of My Sister, St. Thérèse* (authorized translation of CSG).

NPPA   *Notes des Carmelites préparatoires au Procès apostolique de Thérèse.* (Preparatory notes of the Carmelites for the Apostolic Process.)

PA   Procès Apostolique, 1915-1917 (Rome: 1976).

PO   Procès de l'Ordinaire, 1910-1911 (Rome: 1973).

VT   Revue *Vie thérèsienne.* (Magazine *Thérésian Life*).

Writings of St. John of the Cross

A   *The Ascent of Mount Carmel*, in *The Collected Works of St. John of the Cross.*

C   *The Spiritual Canticle*; Thérèse read the B version given in *The Collected Works of St. John of the Cross.* Where this translation differs from the French text cited by the author, CSB will indicate the copy that Thérèse used.

F   *The Living Flame of Love* in *The Collected Works of St. John of the Cross.* Where this translation or numbering differs from the French text cited by the author, VFA will indicate the copy that Thérèse used.

N   *The Dark Night*, in *The Collected Works of St. John of the Cross.*

K-RJ   *The Collected Works of St. John of the Cross.* The levels of division of a work (book, chapter, paragraph number; or stanza, paragraph number) are separated by periods, followed by the page number. For example, N, 2. 5 (K-RJ, p. 401) indicates *The Dark Night*, Book Two, Chapter 5, on p. 401. Successions of references on the same level are separated by commas; hyphens separate continuing numbers.

"Ah! It is incredible how all my hopes have been fulfilled.
When I used to read St. John of the Cross, I begged
God to work out in me what he wrote, that is,
the same thing as though I were to live to be very old;
to consume me rapidly in Love,
and I have been answered!"
(CJ 8.31.9 [HLC, p. 177])

"The most famous of the daughters
of St. John of the Cross..."
Fr. Marie-Eugène of the Child Jesus
(*Je veux voir Dieu*, p. 698)

FOREWORD

T HIS STUDY WAS BORN IN THE COURSE OF THE 4th
centenary of the death of St. John of the Cross, celebrated in 1991.
My Carmelite brothers had asked me to give three conferences about
the influence of the Spanish saint on the life and works of St. Thérèse
of Lisieux.

It seemed to me quite difficult to "hold forth" for three hours
about such a subject. In fact, after working on it, I ended up giving
seven conferences, so abundant was the material. Some day other
people will treat it in a more exhaustive manner; it is a magnificent
subject for a thesis!

My goal is more modest: first to follow historically in the life
of Sr. Thérèse when it was that she studied certain works of the
Spanish Carmelite. And then to shed light on his influence concerning the three theological virtues in the following order: Love, Faith
and Hope, ending with "to die of Love."

I didn't have any preconceived idea when I started this work;
this plan imposed itself by itself.[1] I emphasize the fact that I don't

intend to *compare* the works of these two great saints. I want only to make evident the influence of the Spanish "father" on his French "daughter."

Soon we will celebrate another centenary: Thérèse's "entering into life" (LT 244 [GC II, p. 1128]) on September 30, 1897. I offer these pages to her in homage for all she has given us, is giving and will give to the Church and to the world.

Guy Gaucher

---

[1] After the fact, this plan turns out to be faithful to the thinking of St. John of the Cross, who ascribes an essential place to the three theological virtues (especially in A, 2). The three always go together (A, 2. 24. 8 [K-RJ, p. 243]). The Spanish Carmelite has attributed a color to each one: white for faith, green for hope and red for charity (N, 2. 21. 3 [K-RJ, p. 446]).

JOHN AND THÉRÈSE: FLAMES OF LOVE

1

FROM LES BUISSONETS
TO THE INFIRMARY OF CARMEL…

> *"Ah! how many lights have I not drawn*
> *from the works of our holy Father,*
> *St. John of the Cross!"*
>
> Thérèse (Ms A, p. 179 [83rº])

ALL THE ARTICLES WE HAVE BEEN ABLE TO CON-
sult concerning the influence of St. John of the Cross on Sr. Thérèse
of the Child Jesus obviously quote the famous sentence in her first
manuscript: "Ah! how many lights have I not drawn from the works
of our holy Father, St. John of the Cross! At the ages of seventeen
and eighteen, I had no other spiritual nourishment..." (Ms A, p. 179
[83r°]).

Before commenting on these lines, we must read the continu-
ation of the quote: "...later on, however, all books left me in aridity
and I'm still in that state." Sr. Thérèse adds that in her "helpless-
ness, Holy Scripture and the Imitation come to my aid (...). But it
is especially the *Gospels* that sustain me during my hours of prayer,
for in them I find what is necessary for my poor little soul."

Usually people deduce from this passage that the influence of
St. John of the Cross touched Thérèse only during those two years
(1890-1891) and that afterwards she freed herself from it. A simple
chronology shows not only that she did no such thing, but that the

influence of St. John of the Cross actually stayed with her until her death.

In this first chapter I want to demonstrate with the help of factual texts and testimonies that the Spanish Carmelite profoundly impregnated the life, thinking and attitudes of the young Lisieux Carmelite throughout her life as a religious.

* * *

We would like to begin by recalling some facts that are still too little known concerning the place of St. John of the Cross in France in the 19th century and especially in Carmel.

We have received sufficient information about this subject from the remarkable study by André Bord, *Saint Jean de la Croix en France*,[1] which dispenses us from having to carry out any other historical exploration.

I have taken what Msgr. Saudreau, an historian of spirituality, has written: "The Spanish author was still regarded as an obscure author at the end of the century; he was little read and one almost never saw him quoted as an authority."[2]

André Bord can support this statement quite broadly. It is sufficient to borrow some of his conclusions.

In the 18th century, "the influence [of John of the Cross] seems to have ceased abruptly. The condemnation of Fénelon[3] in 1699 — shortly after John was beatified in 1675 and prior to his canonization in 1726 — had an almost fatal effect, not only on all kinds of distorted spiritual movements but also on mysticism itself, throughout the entire 18th century. For example, the translation of the poetry of St. John of the Cross by the 17th century Carmelite brother

---

[1] André Bord, *Saint Jean de la Croix en France* [St. John of the Cross in France], Beauchesne, 1993.

[2] *La Spiritualité moderne* [Modern Spirituality], Bloud and Gay, 1940, p. 82.

[3] [François Fénelon (1651-1715), French priest and writer (*The Adventures of Telemachus*, 1699) who favored education based on learning experience versus scholarly studies. He was the educator of the grandson of Louis XIV; he became very unpopular after his publications and retreated from public life — Trans.]

Cyprian of the Birth of the Virgin, had to wait almost three centuries before it was republished. Nevertheless it existed in libraries; around 1910, Valéry and Baruzi[4] would discover and pay tribute to it. At the end of the 19th century, we note a reawakening. After the new editions and the publication of Maillard's translation by Migne,[5] a bishop by the name of Gilly made his own translation, just as the Carmelites in Paris [in their 3rd centenary translation] were referring to Thérèse of the Child Jesus as the daughter of St. John of the Cross, thereby fostering continuous faithfulness to the mystical doctor."[6]

It still remained that the Christian population "at large" did not know St. John of the Cross. But within the French Carmels, whence came this ignorance of one of the masters of the Carmelite Reform?

It can be assumed that at the beginning of the Carmelites' presence in France in 1608, Cardinal de Bérulle's[7] decision to distance the friars from the nuns, contrary to St. Teresa's wishes, was the reason for their nescience of St. John of the Cross. Consequently, the "spiritual sap" of his teachings and influence dried up somewhat in the French branches of Carmel.

If we focus our attention on the Carmel of Lisieux in the last

---

4   [Well-known French authors who wrote a very significant thesis about John of the Cross in the early 1920's — Trans.]
5   [19th-century French editor in Paris who edited the works of the Church Fathers in 400 volumes — Trans.]
6   *Op. cit.,* pp. 230-231.
7   Cf. S.-M. Morgain, *Pierre de Bérulle et les Carmelites de France* [Pierre de Bérulle and the Carmelites of France], Cerf, 1995, 592 pages. [Cardinal de Bérulle, 1575-1629, was a French Carmelite who played a major role in introducing the Teresian Carmel into France from Spain. Working on the reform of Catholicism in France, he considered the Spanish Carmelites an excellent instrument to help that cause. He was so persistent in bringing the Teresian nuns to his country that he himself traveled with six Discalced Carmelites from Spain, who knew St. Teresa of Avila, to Paris. Contrary to the wishes of St. Teresa, he separated the friars from the nuns and became the Superior General of the Oratory and the official visitator for the nuns in France. Two of the nuns, Sr. Ann of Jesus and Bl. Ann of Bartholomew, disagreed with that development and left for the Spanish Netherlands. Bérulle formed the French nuns in his own spirit, and at his death left 43 Carmels in France — Trans.]

quarter of the 19th century, we ask ourselves who could have profited from reading the works of John of the Cross? The entire community (26 Sisters) read relatively little. We should not forget that education for French women at the end of the 19th century remained very limited.

St. John of the Cross is a difficult author. His reputation as a "mystical" author in a country that — since the Bossuet-Fénelon disputes[8] of the 17th century — dreads "illuminism,"[9] hardly favored an approach of confidence. The Spanish saint was venerated as the inseparable companion of Mother Teresa of Avila, but he was scarcely known.[10]

However, as the year 1891 approached, how could the 3rd centenary of the death of the great Spanish saint not be celebrated? On this occasion, an edition of his works came out and the Lisieux Carmel acquired the volumes from the "Paris Carmelites."[11]

The Lisieux Carmel participated in the commemorative celebrations in its own way. At that time, the saint's feast day was celebrated on November 24. On this day in 1891, Msgr. Flavien Hugonin, bishop of Bayeux and Lisieux, came in order to conclude a retreat given at the Lisieux Carmel on November 22, 23, 24, by Fr. Déodat de Basly, who was invited in from Rennes.[12] Entering the enclosure, the bishop found the young Thérèse who had visited

---

[8] [Disputes between the monarchy as a political structure legitimized by divine law (advocated by Jacques Bossuet, 1627-1704, French theologian and historian) and spirituality based on personal experience (advocated by Fénelon, French poet and priest [see note 3]). Bossuet and Fénelon embodied the two counter-trends at the court of Louis XIV. The clash between proponents of both sides continued in ongoing debate even into the 20th century — Trans.]

[9] [In the 16th and 17th centuries, "illuminism" referred to a variety of unorthodox mysticism. In the 18th century, the name was also used by a political movement whose goal was to promote the Enlightenment in opposition to the monarchy — Trans.]

[10] A very telling anecdote: When Fr. Henri Grialou (age 28) entered the novitiate of the Carmelites of Avon in 1922, the novice master took away the copy of the works of St. John of the Cross that he had brought. But seeing the book annotated in detail, he returned it to him.

[11] An edition begun in 1875 by Douniol and Co.

[12] Cf. *Livres des fondations du carmel de Lisieux* [Book of the foundations of the Carmel of Lisieux], vol. III, p. 177.

him in Bayeux four years earlier to ask to enter Carmel at the age of 15.[13] Let her own words describe this encounter: "The Bishop… was always kind to me…. I remember especially his visit on the occasion of our Father St. John of the Cross's Centenary. He took my head in his hands and gave me a thousand caresses; never was I so honored!"[14]

It would be interesting to know what the conferences by Fr. Déodat de Basly were about during those three days. We want to point out that on November 23, Msgr. Hugonin attended the conference of Fr. Vallée, O.P.[15] who was giving a retreat at the Carmel in Caen. Lethielleux published these texts in 188 pages. I simply want to emphasize — and it is very revealing — that the Dominican summarized *The Ascent of Mount Carmel* and *The Dark Night*, ignoring the *Spiritual Canticle* and *The Living Flame of Love*. The field of ascetic doctrine was still reserved for a few, according to the thinking of the time.

Let us get back to young Sr. Thérèse in the Carmel of Lisieux. The same day, November 24, she "draws out by lot" from a basket — according to an old Carmelite custom — a paper on which the testament of St. John of the Cross could be read: "My daughter, I leave you my interior annihilation. The soul who wills to possess God totally must renounce all in order to give herself totally to this great God!…"[16] For this feast she and her Sister companions had prepared holy cards, some of which incorporated relics.[17]

It should be emphasized that in this year, 1891, a certain number of bishops submitted a petition to Rome for the Spanish Carmelite to be proclaimed a Doctor of the Church. But the request

---

[13] Cf. Ms A, p. 116 (54v°).

[14] Ms A, p. 156 (72v°) [GC II, p. 737].

[15] This was the Fr. Vallée (1841-1927), a well-known Dominican, who played such an important role in the life of Blessed Elizabeth of the Trinity from the Carmel of Dijon.

[16] GC II, p. 705.

[17] Some examples are in the album of P. Descouvemont-H.N. Loose, *Thérèse et Lisieux* [Thérèse and Lisieux], Cerf, OAA, OCL, Novalis, 1991, pp. 170-173; and, by the same authors, *Sainte Thérèse de Lisieux. La vie en images* [St. Thérèse of Lisieux. Her life in images], 1995, pp. 350-354.

fell through.[18] Is it not telling, to have a saint of this stature sink into oblivion? After all, he had been beatified [1675] and canonized [1726]. What did it take to recognize the great distinction of his doctrine? Thirty-five years were required to achieve this!

As for herself, young Thérèse had no doubt about this matter; she associated herself by prayer with the progress[19] of the cause reported in various publications. It is interesting to point out certain lines in the document of Pius XI, who declared St. John of the Cross a Doctor of the Church on August 24, 1926. He wrote: "Since 1891, on the occasion of the 3rd centenary of his death, several cardinals along with the Spanish clergy insistently beseeched our predecessor Pope Leo XIII to declare St. John of the Cross a Doctor of the Church. After that, the deans of Catholic universities and superiors of religious communities also pleaded incessantly about this matter to the Holy See."

When Thérèse recalled being "17 and 18," this corresponds precisely with the years 1890 and 1891. She made her profession on September 8, 1890, and 1891 (with the retreat by Fr. Alexis Prou in October) was an important year in her spiritual life, as we will see. It is precisely in those years that she says she nourished herself with the works of St. John of the Cross, to the great astonishment of her friends. Two testimonies give evidence of this. Sr. Marie of the Angels, novice mistress, declared at the Apostolic Process: "Above all she loved the Holy *Gospel*, holy books, the *Song of Songs*, the works of St. John of the Cross. I think she was only 17 when she spoke to me about certain passages of his mysticism with an intelligence so far beyond her age, that I was completely amazed."[20] And Mother Agnès of Jesus reported that Mother Hermance of the Heart of Jesus

---

[18] Fr. S.-J. Piat, *Saint Jean de la Croix et la belle aventure thérésienne* [St. John of the Cross and the wonderful Thérésian adventure], VT 19, July 1965, p. 150.

[19] Sr. Marie of the Trinity, VT 77, p. 50. Cf. the book by R.F. Alphonse Marie of Jesus, *Vie de saint Jean de la Croix* [Life of St. John of the Cross], Lyon, Vitte, 1891, translated from Italian by Fr. Feige; the appendix was intended to promote the cause for St. John of the Cross as a Doctor of the Church, pp. 112-114.

[20] PA, p. 350.

said: "One day during her novitiate, Sr. Thérèse of the Child Jesus spoke in recreation about the doctrine of St. John of the Cross with an elderly nun who had been prioress of the Carmel of Coutances. The nun later said to me with astonishment: 'How is it possible that a child of 17 understands these things and discusses them in such a way! This is admirable, I can't get over it.'"[21]

With even greater reason the other Carmelites couldn't "get over it," because several of them had surely never read the author of *The Living Flame.*

"To suffer and to be despised"

When did Thérèse Martin encounter St. John of the Cross? It seems very unlikely that she hadn't heard about him in her family at Les Buissonets, especially since two of her sisters had entered Carmel: Pauline on October 2, 1882, and Marie on October 15, 1886.

In the evenings at Les Buissonets they were reading *The Liturgical Year* by Dom Guéranger. The volumes were purchased as they appeared in print. In the sixth volume we find the life of St. John of the Cross. Furthermore, Thérèse could find some teachings about the Carmelite in the pages of Fr. Bourbonne.[22]

One of Céline's comments is very precious: "Since her adolescence, how often she would enthusiastically repeat these words of St. John of the Cross: 'Lord, to suffer and be despised for you!' That was the theme of our aspirations, when at the belvédère window we would talk together about eternal life."[23]

Thérèse's memory was full of those evenings in the belvédère during the summer of 1887; she was 14½, Céline 18. This is how

---

[21] Mother Agnès of Jesus, NPPA, concerning the subject of Sr. Thérèse's "reputation of sanctity" during and after her life, CG I, p. 543 [French edition].

[22] *Petites Fleurs ou Extraits de la doctrine et la vie des saints et des auteurs approuvés* [Little Flowers or Excerpts of the doctrine and life of the saints and of approved authors], GC I, p. 634, and DE 7.16.3 [HLC, p. 101].

[23] MSG, pp. 14-15.

she recalls them in 1895, precisely in a spirit characteristic of St. John of the Cross:

"Jesus, wanting us to advance together, formed bonds in our hearts stronger than blood. He made us to become *spiritual sisters*, and in us were realized the words of St. John of the Cross's Canticle (speaking to her Spouse, the bride exclaims):

> Following Your footprints
> Maidens run lightly along the way;
> The touch of a spark,
> The special wine,
> Cause flowings in them from the balsam of God.

"Yes, it was very *lightly* we followed in Jesus' footprints. The sparks of love He sowed so generously in our souls, and the delicious and strong wine He gave us to drink made all passing things disappear before our eyes, and from our lips came aspirations of love inspired only by Him. How sweet were the conversations we held each evening in the belvédère!"[24]

For her part Céline, who became Sr. Geneviève, having read those lines of her young sister, gives her version like this:

"Those conversations in the belvédère have left such profound memories that I recall them as if it were yesterday. What Thérèse has written about them in the *Story of a Soul*, far from being exaggerated, seems to me to fall short of the actual reality. (...) Often we started out by reciting with incredible ardor those words of St. John of the Cross that enflamed us with desire and love: 'Lord! To suffer and to be despised for you.' Yes, we long for this with all our might."[25]

Later, when Thérèse will speak with Céline in the parlor of Carmel about the trials of their humiliated father, who was at the

---

[24] Ms A, p. 103 (47v°/48r°), quoting C, sta. 25 [cf. K-RJ, p. 569]. In these quotations, the emphases are those of Thérèse.

[25] MSG, p. 17.

time a resident in the hospital of the Bon Saveur in Caen, she will remember their conversations in the belvédère:
"Who could express the visits we had together? Ah! far from separating us, Carmel's grilles united our souls more strongly; we had the same thoughts, the same desires, the same *love for Jesus* and *for souls*. When Céline and Thérèse were speaking together, never did a word concerning the things of the earth mingle in their conversations which were already in the heavens. As formerly in the *belvédère*, they dreamed about things of *eternity*. To enjoy this endless happiness as soon as possible, they chose as their lot here on earth both *suffering* and *contempt*" (Ms A, p. 157 [73v°]). Here again is the famous saying of St. John of the Cross, already mentioned: "To suffer and to be despised."

At the age of 13, young Thérèse had written these words in fine lettering on February 8, 1886, on a page of handwriting exercises done at the school of Notre-Dame du Pré. Fr. Emmanuel Renault has emphasized the importance of this discovery.[26] Had the young student copied this text or had she herself composed those words? It needs to be noticed that she wrote, "Lord, to suffer and to be despised," putting the verb in the feminine gender.[27] This affirmation was not unfamiliar to her. She who constantly frequented the *Imitation of Christ* and knew its paragraphs by heart, had read: "Jesus Christ wanted to suffer and to be despised" (II, 1:5). But it must be said that this assertion is the best known of the entire work of St. John of the Cross. Let us recall its origin.

One day John of the Cross, prior of Segovia, saw an image of Christ that had been thrown out. He brought it into the church.

---

[26] "Presence de saint Jean de la Cross dans la vie et les écrits de sainte Thérèse de l'Enfant-Jésus" ["Presence of St. John of the Cross in the life and writings of St. Thérèse of the Child Jesus"], *Carmel*, 1990/3, p. 4. The manuscript disappeared in the fire at the Benedictine monastery of Notre-Dame du Pré (June 1944), but Carmel had a duplicate photocopy of it.

[27] [In French the adjectival ending always identifies the gender of the person indicated; "despised" (*méprisée*, fem.) would have been *méprisé* (masc.) if Therese had merely been quoting St. John of the Cross's text — Trans.]

Once when he was praying before it, he heard these words: "Br. John, ask of me what you desire; I will grant it to you because of this homage you have given me." And the saint answered: "Lord, what I want You to give me is trials to suffer for You, to be despised and esteemed as of little worth."[28]

Without doubt there are no other words of St. John of the Cross better known than these are. Not without humor, an elderly Carmelite nun said to me one day: "In all those decades and years of celebrating the feast of St. John of the Cross, I heard preaching only about 'To suffer and to be despised.' It might well be that our preachers who aren't Carmelites don't know anything more about our Father!"

It seems to have been the same at the time of Sr. Thérèse of the Child Jesus. How many images of John of the Cross had she not seen bearing the famous phrase![29] This was also the case with the edition of the Carmelites of Paris, with an introduction by Fr. Chocarne (1877). It had a picture of the saint on the flyleaf with the subtitle, "Lord, to suffer and to be despised for you!" In 1891 Thérèse herself had painted some of these images, which were sold at the portress office of Carmel.

Fr. Renault has analyzed how and why this austere saying of the Spanish saint affected the young Thérèse.[30] Everything that she had experienced — from the age of four and a half when she lost her mother, until her conversion on Christmas night in 1886 — had made her follow a path of various sufferings. There were the losses of her sisters who entered Carmel one after the other (Pauline and

---

[28] Fr. Crisogono de Jesús Sacramentado, *Vida de san Juan de la Cruz* [Life of St. John of the Cross], Madrid, 1982, 2nd ed., p. 354, with about 15 instances of this fact [cf. Ms A, p. 157, note 190]. Cf. Fr. M. de Goedt, *Documents Épiscopats* [Episcopal Documents], December 1990, p. 7: "Christ's words at Segovia to St. John of the Cross were one of the preferred iconographic themes of painters and engravers." There are some examples in the collected book *Dieu parle dans la nuit* [God speaks in the night], Teresiane Arenzano, ed., 1991, pp. 338-339.

[29] Cf. *Thérèse et Lisieux*, pp. 170-173, for some illustrated examples. Carmel was working for Déduit publishers in Caen.

[30] *Art. cit.*, pp. 8-11.

then Marie), her serious illness at the age of ten (healed by the Virgin's smile on May 13, 1883), and her crisis of scruples for 17 months. Great graces also marked this way: first communion, fusion of love with Jesus at age 11 (May 8, 1884); confirmation received as the "sacrament of Love" (June 14, 1884); graces of prayer and above all the "little miracle" of her healing at Christmas 1886. Freed from everything, ready for the battle to enter Carmel, she received a great grace that suggested her vocation to her one Sunday in July 1887, in the cathedral of St. Peter. While contemplating an image of Christ on the cross, she resolved "to remain in spirit at the foot of the Cross" in order to gather the blood that drips from his wounds and to give it to souls (Ms A, p. 99 [45v°]). She was 14½. Such is the definitive vocation of this teenager who was already conscious of so many interior experiences that she wrote, "what I suffered I shall not be able to say except in heaven!" (Ms A, p. 67 [31r°]).

How can it be astonishing then that the phrase of St. John of the Cross struck her to the point that she could attribute it to herself: "To suffer and to be despised!" in the footsteps of her Beloved Jesus.

Thérèse in Carmel

Having entered Carmel on April 9, 1888, Thérèse Martin later recognized that her "first steps met with more thorns than roses! Yes, suffering opened wide its arms to me and I threw myself into them with love..." (Ms A, p. 149 [69v°]). In the warming room she saw a statue of the Spanish saint embracing a large cross.[31]

For the first feast of the Reformer of Carmel, November 24, 1888, she drew from the basket a note that she recopied and put in her *Christian Manual,* one of the books under her pillow. It said: "My daughter, I leave you my purity of intention!... Imitate me in depriving yourself for God of all consolation and in inclining your

---

[31] Photo in *Thérèse et Lisieux*, p. 171, and our cover.

heart to always choose everything that is least flattering to your taste, whether the choices come from God or from creatures!... This is what is truly called love of God!"[32]

But the great trial of the postulant and then of the novice was still to come. She will be pierced to the core by her love for her father. The humiliation of Louis Martin, first ill, then hospitalized at the Bon Saveur in Caen (February 12, 1889), would be shared by the whole family and foremost by his "little Queen." The "suffering and being despised" became the destiny of the father and his youngest daughter. She had wanted to suffer and be despised, and she was heard! "I recall that in the month of June 1888, at the moment of our first trials, I said: 'I am suffering very much, but I feel I can still bear greater trials.' I was not thinking then of the ones reserved for me. I didn't know that on February 12, a month after my reception of the Habit, our dear Father would drink the *most bitter* and the *most humiliating* of all chalices. Ah! that day I didn't say I was able to suffer more!" (Ms A, pp. 156-157 [73rº]).

She had just completed her full religious name. Since January 10, Sr. Thérèse of the Child Jesus was also called "of the Holy Face," referring to the Suffering Servant in Isaiah 53. The "passion" (Ms A, p. 156 [73rº]) of her father brought her back to the Passion of Jesus. Several days later she wrote to Céline: "Yes, *darling* of my heart, Jesus is there with his cross! (...) To suffer and to be *despised*! ... what *bitterness* but what glory!" (LT 81).

On September 8, 1890, she made her solemn profession, holding on her heart a note addressed to Jesus: "May I never seek nor find anything but yourself alone. May creatures be nothing for me and may I be nothing for them, but may you, Jesus, be *everything*!..." (Pri 2).

The dialectic of St. John of the Cross, of *nothing* and *everything*, was already so very present to her.

---

[32] Œ/T, p. 1231.

"On the waves of confidence and love"

Thérèse was now 17 in 1890, the era of reading John of the Cross, according to her own testimony already quoted. The question clearly poses itself: what did she read of the Spanish Carmelite, and in which edition?

As far as books are concerned, the answer is relatively simple. Sr. Thérèse had access to the edition of the Carmelites in Paris.[33] But having taken a look at these basic texts, we still have to be cautious, knowing that Thérèse always profited from everything that fell into her hands: the text of a picture, a calendar, a reading, an anthology. We will see, in time, the capital importance of the notebooks that her sister Céline brought when she entered Carmel on September 14, 1894.

This is the occasion to mention something about spiritual reading at Carmel at the time of Thérèse. The Sisters had only two hours for personal reading each day, one at noon, the other at 8 p.m. Later (in 1893), Thérèse would often have to use this "free time" to compose poetry, theater pieces, and write her manuscript "out of obedience." This free time was thus very limited.

On the other hand, the kind of reading was not at all "academic." Thérèse's readings were not systematic, and scrupulously critical thinking did not encumber her respect for the text. She took very few — if any — notes, and when she copied a passage she didn't hesitate to change a punctuation mark or a word (conforming to the usage of her time).[34] She had great freedom and took whatever liberties she needed.

Since nothing is really methodical for her in this respect, it is very difficult to say whether she truly read the works of St. John of the Cross.

---

[33] Cf. Bibliography, pp. 166-167.

[34] "Thus the Jesuit Marcel Bouix (1806-1889) published a major translation in 1854. Unfortunately he was more worried about elegance than concerned for fidelity; without saying so, he suppressed more or less lengthy passages, sometimes whole chapters" (Bord, *Jean de la Croix en France* [John of the Cross in France], p. 137).

In going back to the index of quotations in the *Collected Works* of Thérèse, we count 105 explicit quotations from St. John of the Cross. There are only five from *The Ascent of Mount Carmel* and two from *The Dark Night*. On the other hand, there are 48 from the *Spiritual Canticle* and 16 from *The Living Flame of Love*. These statistics are striking.[35] We cannot affirm that the young Carmelite truly read the ascetic, more doctrinal, works of the Spanish saint. On the other hand, she had instinctively been drawn to the works that deal with and describe transformative union. Attracted by the Song of Songs,[36] she read the *Spiritual Canticle* with delight[37] and quoted it quite often. To a lesser extent she quoted *The Living Flame of Love*, she who will want to "die of love."

At age 17 and 18, she had no other spiritual nourishment, that much we know for sure; this was mentioned above. No one advised her; it was her admirable intuition — under the movement of the Holy Spirit — that guided her to the final works of the Spanish Carmelite.

Spiritual masters often advised Carmelite novices to "begin with the end."[38] A reader must have understood the splendid sum-

---

[35] Cf. the table in the Appendices, p. 155. Thanks to the Centenary edition (1992), we are slightly modifying E. Renault's statistics, *art. cit.*, pp. 12-15.

[36] Cf. her quotations of it and her commentaries, BT pp. 101-106. She confided to Sr. Marie of the Trinity that if she could have written about anything at all, she would have commented on the Song of Songs (CRM, p. 147; [cf. P. Descouvemont, *Thérèse of Lisieux and Marie of the Trinity: The transformative relationship of St. Therese of Lisieux and her novice, Sister Marie of the Trinity* (New York: Alba House, 1997), p. 66; translation of *Une novice de saint Thérèse. Souvenirs et témoinages de sœur Marie de la Trinité* (Paris: Cerf, 1985) — Trans.].

[37] It should be noted that Thérèse had the good fortune to read the *Spiritual Canticle B*. She had apparently ignored the arguments about these two versions (A and B) of the Canticle. Today both are recognized as authentic. The later version, B, incorporates more detail; in this sense it is fortunate that this was the text Thérèse read in the edition of the Paris Carmelites.

[38] This is also how Fr. Marie-Eugène of the Child Jesus, OCD (1894-1967) advised the members of the secular Institute of Notre-Dame de Vie: "When you read our Father St. John of the Cross, you must begin with *The Living Flame of Love*" (November 5, 1966). Cf. *Jean de la Croix, présence de lumière* [John of the Cross, presence of light], published by Carmel, 1991, p. 164. Fr. Victor Sion, OCD (d. 1990), novice master of the Paris province for 24 years, gave the same advice.

mits of the *Spiritual Canticle* and *The Living Flame* in order to have the courage to go further. Only the desire to arrive at the summit allows austere means to be used without getting discouraged, when stumbling upon the stones of *The Ascent* and facing the obscurities of *The Dark Night*.

We return to Sr. Thérèse in 1890-1891. A much later testimony of Céline's throws light upon her younger sister's development. "At this time and even later, she particularly liked the works of St. John of the Cross. When I had joined her again in the monastery (9/14/1894), I witnessed her enthusiasm when, looking at the text of our Blessed Father in *The Ascent of Mount Carmel*, she stopped and made me pay attention to the line where he writes, 'Here, there is no longer any way, because for the just man there is no law.' She was then breathless from emotion to convey her happiness. This saying helped her very much *to take her own liberties in her explorations of pure love*, which some people judged as presumption. She applied all her boldness to find and attain an entirely new *way*, that of spiritual childhood. There is only one such way, that's how straight and short it is, ending up *in one go* at the very heart of God. I believe that all her prayers aimed solely at this study about the 'science of love.'"[39]

It is true that Sr. Thérèse at age 17-18 was searching for her path. She hadn't found a way of inner growth and fulfillment in the prevailing spirituality of her Carmel. She remained rather alone, still occasionally scrupulous. A certain rigorous atmosphere weighed heavily on her. Her spiritual father, Fr. Pichon, S.J., left for Canada. She wrote to him every month. Overwhelmed with mail, he wrote back... when he could. Fr. Youf, chaplain and regular confessor of the nuns, was good, but scrupulous and fearful. Communications between Thérèse and Monsieur Delatroëtte, superior of Carmel, hadn't warmed up since his resolute opposition to the entry of this much-too-young girl into Carmel.

---

[39] CSG, 1952. 1st ed., pp. 203-205. This text disappeared in subsequent editions [cf. K-RJ, p. 111].

The novice had indeed met "a saint" in her community, a saint who was "made holy by the practice of... the ordinary virtues." "Ah! that type of sanctity seems the *truest* and the *most holy* to me, and it is the type that I desire because in it one meets with no deceptions" (Ms A, pp. 169-170 [78r°]).

In the memoirs Thérèse wrote about Mother Geneviève, we see the young Claire Bertrand praying a novena to St. John of the Cross and receiving many perceptible graces from it.[40]

However, Mother Geneviève offered herself to the justice of God on Good Friday, 1890. She had lived in the infirmary for years, enduring many great sufferings. On Sundays, young Thérèse went to see her and joyfully received her spiritual bouquets (Ms A, p. 169 [78r°]).

Nevertheless their paths were going to part. "Mother Geneviève herself, to whom the saint [Thérèse], still a postulant, had revealed her project of perfection and the intensity of her need to love, was a little frightened by this audacity, which was unusual for a beginner, to tell the truth. It was at this point that she thought to discretely alert Sr. Agnès of Jesus, urging her to caution her young sister against illusions and to restrain a confidence that she considered exaggerated."[41]

Mother Geneviève died after much suffering, on December 5, 1891, several days after the festivities of the 3rd centenary of the death of St. John of the Cross. These celebrations took place a little after the community retreat of October 8-15, which was to be preached by a Franciscan Father. Unable to come, he delegated a fellow friar, Fr. Alexis Prou. Thérèse, always fearful of retreats,[42] made a prepa-

---

[40] Œ/T, p. 1219.

[41] Fr. S.-J. Piat, *À la découverte de la voie d'enfance* [Discovery of the Way of Childhood], published by the Franciscans, 1964, p. 113.

[42] "She suffered a lot when they were speaking in the conferences about how easily one can fall into mortal sin, even by a simple thought. It seemed so difficult to her to offend God when one loves him. During the whole course of these exercises, I used to see her pale and distraught; she could no longer eat or sleep, and she would have fallen sick if this had lasted" (Mother Agnès of Jesus, PA, p.163).

ratory novena. Against all expectation, Fr. Alexis Prou's direction completely freed her from that fear. A single encounter was sufficient.

"The year that followed my Profession, that is, two months before Mother Geneviève's death, I received great graces during my retreat. Ordinarily the retreats that are preached are more painful to me than the ones I make alone, but this year it was otherwise. I had made a preparatory novena with great fervor, in spite of the inner sentiment I had, for it seemed to me that the preacher would not be able to understand me since he was supposed to do good to great sinners but not to religious souls. God wanted to show me that He was the Director of my soul, and so He made use of this Father specifically, who was appreciated only by me..." (Ms A, p. 173 [80r°/ v°]).

At a time when she was restrained on all sides,[43] here is a priest who launched her "upon the waves of *confidence and love*" [Ms A, p. 174 (80v°)]. It was October 1891. These dates coincide with her reading of St. John of the Cross. The encouragement of the Franciscan was providential. "At this decisive moment, she found in the Saint's treatises the light, energy, the audacious confidence which allow her to throw herself on the waves of love."[44] This path is the one of St. John of the Cross. Furthermore, Thérèse quotes him:

> ...with no other light or guide
> than the one that burned in my heart.
> This guided me
> more surely than the light of noon
> to where he was awaiting me
> — him I knew so well....[45]

---

[43] By Fr. Blino, S.J., for example, the occasional preacher, attempting to restrain her desires for sanctity (GC I, p. 621, note 8, concerning LT 107).

[44] Fr. Marie-Eugène of the Child Jesus, *Triduum saint Jean de la Croix* [St. John of the Cross Triduum], 1927, p. 52.

[45] Ms A, p. 105 (49r°), quoting *The Dark Night*, sta. 3 and 4 (Céline's Notebook, VT 78, p. 152; [cf. K-RJ, p. 359]).

Or, what is it that Thérèse later said to her novice, Sr. Marie of the Trinity? "He is the saint of Love par excellence."[46] This Sister testified: "She had a filial affection for our mother St. Teresa and our father St. John of the Cross. The Works of the latter especially enflamed her with love."[47]

Fr. Marie-Eugène has written that Thérèse needed the teachings of the Spanish saint, the light of his experience, in order to be reassured about her own; the light of his principles to illuminate her own path into new areas.[48] Taking support from him, she advanced all alone, driven by the Holy Spirit, on the road that will lead at the end of 1894 and the beginning of 1895, to the discovery of the way of spiritual childhood.[49]

A Hidden Treasure (1892-1893)

Statistics must be looked at with great care. It is true that we find hardly any quotations from St. John of the Cross in the years 1892-1893: a total of six in 21 of Thérèse's letters. But we must read these important letters. Her meditation on John of the Cross didn't stop. It was nourished by correspondence with Céline.

In the summer of 1892, Thérèse's sister was staying with the Guérins in the chateaux of the Musse (near Evreux), where she discovered the splendors of nature. Thérèse wrote to her: "I myself see nothing of all that, but I say with St. John of the Cross, 'My Beloved is the mountains, the lonely, wooded valleys, etc.'"[50] In her response, Céline in turn referred to the *Gloss on the Divine* and to

---

[46] VT 77, p. 50.

[47] PO, p. 462.

[48] *Under the Torrent of His Love: Thérèse of Lisieux, a Spiritual Genius*, p. 99.

[49] Cf. C. De Meester, *Dynamique de la confiance. Genèse et structure de la voie de "l'enfance spirituelle" chez sainte Thérèse de Lisieux*, Cerf, 1969. A new updated edition, 1995 [*The Power of Confidence. Genesis and structure of the "way of spiritual childhood" of St. Thérèse of Lisieux*, New York: Alba House, 1998].

[50] LT 135 [GC II, p. 752], quoting C, sta. 14.

the *Spiritual Canticle*.[51] In October, Thérèse quoted the *Prayer of the Soul enkindled by love*: "Then we could say with St. John of the Cross, 'All is mine, all is for me, the earth is mine, the heavens are mine, God is mine, and the Mother of my God is mine.'"[52]

When she celebrated Céline's 24th birthday in April 1893, she meditated on the "drop of dew," so small, apparently so useless. St. John of the Cross had also spoken about it: "[God] in the omnipotence of his fathomless love absorbs the soul in himself more efficaciously and forcibly than a torrent of fire would devour a drop of morning dew that usually rises and dissolves in the air."[53]

This theme returned on July 6, with another quotation from the Spanish Carmelite: "Jesus is teaching her to learn 'to draw profit from everything, *from the good* and *the bad* she finds in herself.'"[54]

Céline's response, again from the Musse the following year, recalled the time when "…so transported, so strong, so courageous, I used to read St. John of the Cross and I was flying so high, my soul filled with joy! The time is past for 'weaving garlands with flowers and emeralds chosen on cool mornings'…" And Céline continued commenting on this stanza 30 of the *Spiritual Canticle*, then recalled the bouquet tied "with a single hair."

She had begun her letter like this: "Within me, there is always nothing, always the dark night."[55] From the easy flow of this correspondence, we realize how readily the two sisters nourished their exchanges with the thoughts of St. John of the Cross. Often they understood each other by a half-spoken word.

In the course of the summer 1893, when she wrote letters to Céline that are extremely important, Thérèse returned to John of the Cross on August 2: "Jesus is a *hidden* treasure," she said. Or, "To

---

[51] LC 149 [GC II, p. 755], quoting C, sta. 14.

[52] LT 137 [GC II, p. 761].

[53] C, commentary on sta. 31, vol. II, p. 17, in Thérèse's edition [cf. K-RJ, p. 596]. Thérèse's letter is LT 141.

[54] LT 142, quoting *A Gloss (with a spiritual meaning)* [cf. K-RJ, p. 70]. Thérèse will take up this text again in Ms A, p. 179 (83r°), and in her poem PN 30 [*Poems*, p. 148].

[55] LC 154 [GC II, p. 798].

find a hidden thing one must hide oneself...." She had read these lines in the explanation of the first verse of stanza 1 of the *Spiritual Canticle*.[56]

In October for Céline's feast, we can find a possible reminiscence in her sister's letter: "Everything brings us to Jesus. The flowers growing on the edge of the road do not captivate our hearts."[57] This refers to "I will not gather flowers" in the *Spiritual Canticle*.[58]

To Léonie, who took the habit at the Visitation in Caen on April 6, 1894, Thérèse also wrote: "Jesus... is saying to you as to the spouse of the Canticle: 'You have wounded my heart, my sister, my spouse, by one of your eyes and by one strand of your hair fluttering on your neck.'" This passage from the Song of Songs (4:9) had been commented on by John of the Cross.[59]

So the trace of the Castilian poet remained during these years, even if we can refer to only a few documents. But they are of great significance, as Fr. De Meester has shown.

Céline's Notebooks (1894–1895)

But here the correspondence with Céline is going to cease. Louis Martin died at the Musse on July 29, 1894. Céline, who had stayed with him until the end, was now free to realize her call to Carmel. On September 14, she arrived at the monastery. In her luggage, besides her massive camera equipment, she carried the notebooks she had filled in the course of her studies. At the Guérins she had been able to copy passages from the Bible; she even had access to two! Behold! This was something that could have made her younger sister "jealous," who was not allowed to study the Old Testament in the novitiate. Thérèse very quickly seized upon these note-

---

[56] LT 145 [GC II, p. 808; [cf. K-RJ, p. 481, par. 9].

[57] LT 149 [GC II, p. 826].

[58] C, 3. 3 [K-RJ, p. 489].

[59] C, sta. 31 [K-RJ, p. 598, par. 10]. LT 164 [GC II, p. 855].

books and, thanks to the masterly study by Fr. Conrad De Meester, we know that she found in them the two texts that would be decisive for the discovery of her way.[60]

But in 1893, "according to all probability," Céline had also copied texts of St. John of the Cross. This fact is of the highest importance to us, for Thérèse would use these notebooks and continually nourish herself from them. Which texts do we find there?[61]

Céline recopied for Thérèse six poems by John of the Cross, using the translation by the Carmelites of Paris (1877):

> — *Stanzas concerning an ecstasy experienced in high contemplation* ("Entréme donde no supe") [cf. K-RJ, pp. 53-54]
> — *Stanzas given a spiritual meaning* ("Tras de un amoroso lance") [cf. K-RJ, pp. 56-57]
> — *A gloss (with spiritual meaning)* ("Sin arrimo y con arrimo") [cf. K-RJ, p. 70]
> — *Stanzas of the Soul* (taken from *The Dark Night*) [cf. K-RJ, pp. 358-359]
> — *Stanzas between the Soul and the Bridegroom* (taken from the *Spiritual Canticle*) [cf. K-RJ, pp. 471ff.]
> — *The Living Flame of Love* [cf. K-RJ, pp. 52-53].

In addition there were some brief selections from St. John of the Cross's *Letters* and *Precautions*. It is evident that Thérèse generously drew upon the treasures of this notebook. We can't underestimate its importance because Thérèse used it when, in obedience to Mother Agnès of Jesus, she undertook writing her first manuscript in January 1895. Numerous references to John of the Cross come from this notebook.[62]

In 1895, Thérèse received an edition of *Maxims and Spiritual Advice of Our Blessed Father St. John of the Cross*, published by the

---

[60] *The Power of Confidence*, 1998 [translation of the 1995 French edition], pp. 29ff.

[61] This will take us back to VT 78, April 1980, pp. 145-160, which reproduces all these texts. On page 147, see an historical introduction by Sr. Cécile, OCD.

[62] Ms A (86 folios) quotes John of the Cross 19 times.

Carmelites of Paris (H. Oudin, 1895), drawn originally from the *Collected Works*. She carefully guarded this for her personal use until the end of her life.[63] In July 1896, she was photographed holding this book in her hands.[64] It contains 108 pages; 365 maxims are given and arranged under 22 headings. At the end (pp. 103-106) is the *Prayer of a Soul Taken with Love* that had made such a profound impression on Thérèse.

Combining these two important sources, Sr. Cécile, OCD,[65] wrote: "this pocket anthology (Céline's notebook) and the book of *Maxims* offered Sr. Thérèse those texts of St. John of the Cross that influenced her the most."[66] This puts into context, as we have emphasized, any theory of a complete and consistent study of the works of the Spanish Carmelite. Thérèse, without doubt, never hampered herself with weighty volumes; she preferred the easy reading of her sister Céline's notebooks.

The crucial testimony of Sr. Marie of the Trinity

On June 16, 1894, Marie Castel entered the Carmel of Lisieux at the age of 20; she became Sr. Marie of the Trinity, Sr. Thérèse's novice (the only one younger than Thérèse in Carmel). The friendship between these two Carmelites was profound and Thérèse did everything in her power to lead Sr. Marie of the Trinity to her profession on April 30, 1896. This was not without difficulties, because the arrival of this young "Parisian," coming from the Carmel of the *rue de Messine* in Paris, didn't win the unanimous support of the Lisieux community.[67]

---

[63] Cf. DE, pp. 844 and 519. The original is found at the Carmel of St.-Flour.

[64] VTL, num. 36; [cf. *Photo Album*, p. 180]. This is our cover photo.

[65] [Sr. Cécile, of the Lisieux Carmel, is *the* leading archivist of Thérèse's writings — Trans.]

[66] VT 78, April 1980, p. 147.

[67] One can read Fr. Descouvemont, *Therese of Lisieux and Marie of the Trinity: The transformative relationship of St. Therese of Lisieux and her novice, Sister Marie of the Trinity.* She was born in Normandy, but had grown up in Paris (1891-1893), from whence she had entered Carmel.

What interests us here is the fact that this novice was a privileged witness concerning the influence of St. John of the Cross on her novice mistress. In this regard, the publication of her notebooks in *Vie thérésienne* constitutes a source of great value that has scarcely been exploited until now,[68] from the point of view that concerns us.

Her important testimony is as follows:

"In our conversations, it was her favorite subject, we came back to it all the time. She quoted from memory, with an indefinable graciousness, very long passages from the holy Doctor, especially the sayings that comforted her in the times of her great trials. Among them was the following: 'O souls who in spiritual matters desire to walk in security and consolation! If you but knew how much it behooves you to suffer in order to reach this security and consolation,… in no way would you look for comfort either from God or from creatures. You would instead carry the cross and… desire to drink the pure gall and vinegar. You would consider it good fortune (to have a share in this)… and patiently and faithfully suffering exterior trials, … you would merit that God fix his eyes on you, and plunge you more profoundly through deeper spiritual trials in order to give you more interior blessings.'[69]

"'Thus,' continued our Saint with heavenly fervor, 'by welcoming suffering we will be given the grace of an even greater suffering, or rather of an even more profound purification in order to arrive at perfect union in love. Ah! When I had understood that, strength was given to me to suffer all.' She found, then, in the work of St. John of the Cross, the strength to suffer and to pass through purifications. This better explains the 'suffering and contempt' (cf. Ms A, p. 157 [73v°]).

---

[68] Texts from the notebooks of Sr. Marie of the Trinity are found in VT:
— the *Red Notebook* (CRM): VT 74 (April 1979), pp. 138-157;
— *Counsels and Reminiscences* (1-30): VT 73 (January 1980), pp. 51-68;
— new *Counsels and Reminiscences* (31-57): VT 77 (January 1980), pp. 47-67.
VT 77, p. 49, gives the location of all the references to St. John of the Cross in the texts of Sr. Marie of the Trinity.

[69] F, commentary on v. 5 of sta. 2 (vol. II, pp. 187-189 of the 1875 edition used by Thérèse) [K-RJ, p. 668, par. 28]. […] Cf. quotation in Ms B, p. 194 (3r°/3v°); Céline's notebook, VT 78, pp. 149-150.

"One day she said to me: 'The only means of making rapid progress on the way of love is to remain very little. Also, I now sing with our Father St. John of the Cross: The lower and more subdued / and abased I became. / I…sank, ah, so low, / *that I was so high, so high, / that I took the prey*'"[70] This is the basis of the little way.

"As a remembrance of my Taking of the Veil (May 7, 1896) she gave me an image of our Father St. John of the Cross, which was the photograph of a painting by her sister, Rev. Mother Agnès of Jesus. Beneath the image she had written: *'Through love*, to suffer and to be despised…'"[71] Let us note Thérèse's very significant addition [*through love*] to the saint's formula that she loved to quote so much during her adolescent years in Les Buissonets. The whole spirituality of Thérèse is expressed in this. With her supreme liberty, she brings to completion her master St. John of the Cross. "And on the back are three thoughts chosen from the writings of our blessed Father" (cf. LT 188).

"For my profession (April 30, 1896), she offered me our Father's *Gloss on the Divine*, which she had transposed into French verse. This made me aware that the thought she liked best was 'Love knows how to use (what power!) / The good and *the bad* it finds in me' (PN 30).

"Being responsible for the hermitage of our Father St. John of the Cross, I had the idea to represent Mount Carmel, including the sentences, as a decoration (an exact copy of the image found in the book *Ascent of Carmel* [cf. K-RJ, pp. 110-111]). Sr. Thérèse of the Child Jesus expressed her total agreement with this. She made me aware of the two sayings she liked the most: 'Here there is no longer any way because for the just man there is no law' [cf. K-RJ, p. 111], and 'Everything has been given to me without seeking it, when I have not wanted it out of self-love.'

---

[70] This whole long quotation from Sr. Marie of the Trinity is in VT 77, pp. 49-50. The last quotation from John of the Cross is in *Poem VI*, K-RJ, p. 57.

[71] See this image in P. Descouvemont-H.N. Loose, *Sainte Thérèse de Lisieux. La vie en images*, Cerf, 1996, p. 350.

"Several months before her sister Céline's entrance into our Carmel, she had asked her to paint for the community a large portrait of our Father St. John of the Cross. This is an oil painting, measuring 37½ in. high and 29½ in. wide.[72]

"Several times she had expressed to me her desire that our Father St. John of the Cross might be declared a Doctor of the Church, so that his Writings would be substantiated for the good of a greater number of souls. I remain convinced that from Heaven she has worked for this glorious and happy result that fulfills the joy of all the sons and daughters of Carmel.[73]

"In the *Spiritual Canticle* she loved to quote to me:

> When you looked at me
> your eyes imprinted your grace in me;
> for this you loved me ardently;
> and thus my eyes deserved
> to adore what they beheld in you.
> Do not despise me;
> for if, before, you found me dark,
> now truly you can look at me
> since you have looked
> and left in me grace and beauty.
> Let us rejoice, Beloved,
> and let us go forth to behold ourselves
> in your beauty…"[74]

In January of 1929, Sr. Marie of the Trinity still remembered these verses of St. John that "Thérèse of the Child Jesus and I so loved to repeat."[75]

---

[72] Each time the nuns entered choir, they passed by a little statue of the saint (VT 77, p. 52, note d). On the map of Carmel (DE, pp. 816-817), it is "A" near "H."

[73] VT 77, p. 50.

[74] Stanzas 32, 33 and the beginning of 36 [K-RJ, p. 476]; VT 77, p. 51.

[75] VT 77, p. 52, note i.

The way of spiritual childhood

This "little way, a way that is very straight, very short, and totally new" (Ms C, p. 207 [2vº]) was crystallized in Thérèse's heart
and thinking at the end of 1894. She reported this inspired discovery to Mother Marie de Gonzague in June 1897 (Ms C, pp. 207-
208 [2]). A crucial insight, germinating for a long time, was going
to blossom within her.

For Thérèse the little way is the flash of Hope that sprang up
from the shock between the infinity of her desire for holiness and
the realistic consciousness of her radical poverty. Cardinal Daniélou
has said that the little way was "the infinity of desire within total
powerlessness."[76]

"The doctrine of spiritual childhood found the powerful frame-
work of its structure only in light of the teaching of the Doctor of
Carmel."[77] In it, the "nothing" that characterizes St. John of the
Cross's spirituality is filled by God's "everything." The Spanish saint's
self-discipline of poverty and privation led him to divine union,
whereas it is littleness that "aspires" to Mercifulness. "We experience such great peace when we're totally poor, when we depend upon
no one except God" (CJ 8.6.4 [HLC, p. 137]).

Thérèse had begun her religious life with a spirit of effort and
a certain exertion of self-will: "I want to be a saint" (LT 45). But
little by little she discovered that she could do nothing; she experienced her radical incapacity. She then entered the "passivity" of which
St. John of the Cross speaks. She wrote: "directors have others advance in perfection by having them perform a great number of acts
of virtue, and they are right; but my director, who is Jesus, teaches
me not to count up my acts. He teaches me to do *all* through love,
to refuse Him nothing, to be content when He gives me a chance of
proving to Him that I love Him. But this is done in peace, in *aban-*

---

[76] Homily given in the infirmary of the Lisieux Carmel (8/21/1969), published in AL num.
    10, October 1969, p. 13.
[77] Fr. Marie-Eugène of the Child Jesus, *Under the Torrent of His Love*, p. 94.

donment, it is Jesus who is doing all in me, and I am doing nothing."[78]

"At first her little way of confidence and perfect abandonment
seems in complete opposition to the harsh and austere way of St.
John of the Cross. Her little way presents itself as sweet and easy.
But Sr. Thérèse of the Child Jesus supports her doctrine of perfect
confidence and total abandonment upon the *nothing* of John of the
Cross. It is there that she found the law of complete detachment
and from this perfect detachment ensues perfect hope and perfect
confidence."[79]

The amazing discovery of the way of spiritual childhood led
her to offer herself to Merciful Love.

The Act of Oblation to Merciful Love
(June 9, 1895)

During Mass on Trinity Sunday, June 9, 1895, Sr. Thérèse was
inspired to offer herself "as a holocaust victim to Merciful Love" (Ms
A, pp. 180-181 [84r°]). This veritable spiritual revolution cut through
the spirituality of her time where "great and generous" souls would
offer themselves as victims to God's justice.

This is not the place to go into detail about the extreme importance of that offering — summit of Sr. Thérèse's spiritual life and
result of her discovery of the way of spiritual childhood. But we
should at least quickly emphasize how present the influence of St.
John of the Cross is in this Act.[80] We can make of it a reading of

---

[78] LT 142 [GC II, p. 796].

[79] Fr. Marie-Eugène of the Child Jesus, *Retraite* [Retreat] given to the Carmel of Périgueux
(1/9-18/1932), "Conférence sur l'Espérance" ["Conference on Hope"], p. 401. André Bord
says quite well: "This little way that is quite straight, quite short, is the experience of what
John of the Cross calls the *nothing* which, without straying to the right or the left, goes
directly to the *everything* (*Jean de la Croix en France*, p. 217).

[80] On the circumstances and consequences of this Act, cf. our article "Centenaire de l'Acte
d'offrande, 9 juin 1895" [Centenary of the Act of Oblation, June 9, 1895] in the special
issue VT 139, 1995.

references from John of the Cross: Thérèse remembered the *Spiritual Canticle* and *The Living Flame* "more by saturation than erudition."[81]

In her offering to the "Blessed Trinity," she offered the merits of the saints, the angels, the Blessed Virgin Mary. We immediately think of John of the Cross's *Prayer of a Soul Taken with Love* [K-RJ, pp. 87-88].

The famous phrase "The more he wants to give, the more he makes us desire," taken from a letter of the Spanish Carmelite to Mother Eleanor of St. Gabriel (7/8/1589; [K-RJ, p. 750]), close to *Maxim 45*, is one of the fundamental elements of Thérèse's thinking. She based her confidence on it and we know she quoted it often.[82] This is a pillar of the support John of the Cross gives to Thérèse.

The "Divine Glance that cleanses" recalls the *Spiritual Canticle*: "For God to look is for him to love" (commentary on stanza 32; [K-RJ, p. 600]). Or again: "God's gaze first purifies the soul, then renders it pleasing to His eyes" (stanza 33), etc.[83]

This fire "consuming all my imperfections like the fire that transforms everything into itself" obviously recalls stanza 26 of the *Spiritual Canticle*: "[There] these herds of imperfection are more easily consumed than are the rust and tarnish of metal consumed by fire" [K-RJ, p. 580].

"When evening comes…" recalls *Maxim 70* [*Sayings of Light and Love 60*, K-RJ, p. 90].

"May… finally cause me to die" goes back to the death of love, to which we will dedicate our last chapter.

"Eternal embrace" evokes mystical marriage, the spiritual marriage of the soul with God.

---

[81] We can go back to the notes in the New Centenary Edition of *Récréations pieuses — Prières 1992* [Recreational Pieces — Prayers 1992], pp. 563-576. Here, the quotation is from p. 563 [*Prayers*, p. 64].

[82] LT 201 [GC II, p. 1015]; Ms C, p. 250 (31r°); LT 253; CJ 7.13.15 [HLC, p. 94]; CJ 7.16.2 [HLC, p. 100]; CJ 7.18.1 [HLC, p. 102]; etc.

[83] [Cf. K-RJ, introduction and commentary on stanza 33, pp. 599-604; *Prayers*, p. 71, note 36 — Trans.]

So, in this fundamental Act of Thérèse's life, the influence of her Father is very easy to find and very fertile.

"My vocation, at last I have found it…"
(September 8, 1896)

In this year, 1896, we notice in Thérèse the persistent presence of the thinking of St. John of the Cross, mainly during the summer,[84] and not without connection to Sr. Marie of the Trinity.

Thérèse experienced great desires that made her suffer during prayer. These sufferings and the reading of two chapters of the second letter of St. Paul to the Corinthians culminated with the discovery of her vocation, expressed in the famous text of September 8:

"O Jesus, my Love… *my vocation*, at last I have found it.… MY VOCATION IS LOVE!

"Yes, I have found my place in the Church and it is You, O my God, who have given me this place; in the heart of the Church, my Mother, I shall be *Love*…" (Ms B, p. 194 [3v°]).

Sr. Thérèse here reached a new summit of her spiritual life, fruit of her offering to Merciful Love on June 9, 1895. And in manuscript B, containing five folios, we find ten citations of St. John of the Cross.

Sr. Marie of the Trinity made her profession on April 30. To her "doll," whom she had guided to this point, Thérèse offered a poem, *A Gloss on the Divine* (PN 30), which was directly inspired by a poem of John of the Cross.[85] Sr. Thérèse carefully wrote the text in calligraphy on the image. Here is the complete text, copied from that of St. John of the Cross found in Céline's notebook:[86]

---

[84] *Récréations pieuses — Prières* [Pious Recreations — Prayers], NEC, p. 603; [*Prayers*, pp. 91ff.].

[85] Note that the title *A Gloss on the Divine* doesn't indicate a special meaning because numerous poems of the Castilian poet are addressed *a lo divino*, "to the divine." Its content transposes a song about ordinary love to a supernatural level of Divine Love. This image can be seen, front and back, in *Therese et Lisieux*, p. 172.

[86] VT 78, p. 150.

A Gloss on the Divine

Written by O[ur] F[ather] St. John of the Cross and put into verse by the littlest of his daughters to celebrate the Profession of her dear Sister Marie of the Trinity and of the Holy Face.

Without support yet with support,
Living without Light, in darkness,
I am wholly being consumed by Love...

1   I have said an eternal goodbye
    To the world (what extreme happiness)!...
    ... Lifted higher than myself,
    I have no other Support than my God.
    And now I proclaim:
    What I value near Him
    Is to see and feel my soul
    Supported without any support!....

2   Though I suffer without Light
    In this life which lasts but a day,
    At least on earth I possess
    The Heavenly life of Love....
    In the way I have to walk,
    Lies more than one danger,
    But for Love I am willing to live
    In exile's Shadows.

3   Love, I have experienced it,
    Knows how to use (what power!)
    The good and the bad it finds in me.
    It transforms my soul into itself.
    This Fire burning in my soul
    Penetrates my heart forever.
    Thus in its delightful flame
    I am being wholly consumed by Love!....

April 30, 1896. Thérèse of the Ch. Jesus, of the Holy Face
rel. carm. ind. [unworthy Carmelite religious]

Several days later (May 7), Sr. Marie of the Trinity took the veil in a public ceremony. Thérèse offered a new image to the professed: a photograph of the saint's portrait painted by Mother Agnès of Jesus. We know that on the front, below the picture, Thérèse wrote: "*Through love,* to suffer and to be despised!" So for this young Sister who had some difficulties with the community, Thérèse again found this phrase from her youth.

On the back, there are three "thoughts from O[ur] F[ather] St. John of the Cross." Thérèse drew them from her book of *Maxims,* which is why we can number them:

— **129** "The affection [for the creature] is purely spiritual if the love of God grows when it grows, or if the love of God is remembered as often as the affection is remembered, or if the affection gives the soul a desire for God — if by growing in one, the soul grows also in the other."

— **103** "He who walks in the love of God seeks neither his own gain nor his reward, but only to lose all things and himself for God..."

— **70** "In the evening of life, they will examine you on love. Learn then to love God as He wills to be loved and forget yourself."[87]

On August 6, Sr. Thérèse composed a significant *Consecration to the Holy Face* (Pri 12). She put great care into the finely written text, alternating between red and black ink. She proposed this consecration to her two novices who, like her, had the name "of the Holy Face": Sr. Geneviève of St. Thérèse (her sister Céline), who was called Marie of the Holy Face when she entered Carmel; and Sr. Marie of the Trinity of the Holy Face. The image was decorated with photographs of the three Carmelites and each one signed her name.[88]

The text is introduced by two quotations from St. John of the Cross: [89]

---

[87] LT 188 [GC II, p. 953]. See the image in *Thérèse et Lisieux,* p. 173.

[88] See *Sainte Thérèse de Lisieux. La vie en images,* pp. 416-417; [also *Prayers,* p. 91].

[89] [The first text given here is from GC II, p. 1129 (LT 245); the second is from *Prayers,* p. 91, where italics indicate red ink — Trans.]

"The smallest movement of pure Love is more useful to the Church than all other works put together.... Thus it is of the greatest importance that our souls be exercised much in *Love* so that being consumed quickly we do not linger long here on earth but soon attain to the vision of *Jesus, Face to Face.*"

The first is taken from the *Spiritual Canticle B*, commentary on stanza 29. Thérèse did not take the last phrase, "put together," from the original. She quoted this passage for the first time, which she would take up in Ms B, p. 197 (4vº), LT 221 and 245. We can see here the translation, into the words of St. John of the Cross, of her discovery in the summer of 1896: "My vocation is Love."

The second quotation comes from *The Living Flame of Love*, stanza 1, explanation of verse 6.[90] Thérèse modified the translation in which she can read: "It is, then, of the greatest importance that the soul exercise herself much in Love in order that, consuming herself rapidly, she hardly stops here below and arrives promptly in seeing her God Face to Face" [GC II, p. 1129].

We quote from the commentary of the New Centenary Edition:[91]

"The juxtaposition of these two quotations is striking, as if the apostolic zeal of lines 8-9, this 'pure Love,' so 'beneficial to the Church,' found its full accomplishment only in the 'Face to Face' of heaven. The greatest service of the Church then, would demand not so much duration 'on earth' as intensity, 'much,' which should 'quickly' lead to boundless fruitfulness after death. This is the germ of the great desire in the winter of 1896-1897. (...) This is the personal message she will want to leave to her three Carmelite sisters (LT 245). (...) We have a new example of the way Thérèse incorporates and reinterprets her sources, including her teacher John of the Cross."

This shows the beautiful liberty of someone who prophesied her posthumous apostolic fertility without any doubt of it, after a "quickly" consumed life that brought her face to Holy Face.

---

[90] Cf. LT 245, of June (?), 1897 [K-RJ, p. 656, par. 34].

[91] RP. Pri, p. 595; [*Prayers*, pp. 95-96].

From exile to the Kingdom (1897)

This is now the last year of Thérèse's life. In the spring of 1897, she became seriously ill. Tuberculosis — not identified at first — had been spreading since 1894. Now Thérèse was forced to abandon community life: she no longer went to pray in choir, no longer went to the refectory, no longer worked with the novices. She was either in her cell or in the garden if the weather was nice.

After July 8, in very grave condition, she was moved to the infirmary on the ground floor. Since April, Mother Agnès of Jesus (her sister Pauline) had been writing down her young sister's words, which are to be found in *Her Last Conversations*.

What interests us here is the presence of St. John of the Cross in the conversations of the two sisters. One most particular subject comes up often: the "death of love" described by the saint and hoped for by Thérèse — will she experience this kind of death? This very important subject will be the material of our fifth chapter.

Another matter is linked to this one: in the infirmary, Thérèse, coughing up blood, reduced and very thin, could barely read or write. Nevertheless is it very revealing to inventory the few books she has at her bedside. We find here the *Spiritual Canticle* and *The Living Flame of Love* bound in a single volume,[92] and always the *Advice and Maxims*.

Unable to read for long, she was content to mark with little crosses in pencil[93] the passages that seemed important to her for the moment of her death. It is clearly crucial to pinpoint these passages, which we will do in the final chapter.

Also, the sick nun recorded on a little Bristol paper bookmark some page numbers and some brief notes concerning her reading of the *Spiritual Canticle*. Here again, it will be important to decipher

---

[92] Cf. DE, p. 843.

[93] It is with this pencil that she finished her last manuscript (Ms C), being unable to write in ink any more after folio 36r° [p. 258]. This pencil was also used for writing to Fr. Bellière on August 10, 1897 (LT 263).

these notations to better penetrate into the depths of the dying nun's soul.[94]

For the time being, notice that Sr. Thérèse was dying accompanied by the writings of St. John of the Cross. The trajectory that we have followed, from Les Buissonets to the infirmary of Carmel, shows a beautiful continuity, even if there are occasional detours. And to situate how deeply the writings of the Spanish Carmelite have affected her, let us quote only two statements from *Her Last Conversations*:

"With what longing and what consolation I repeated from the beginning of my religious life these other words of St. John of the Cross: 'It is of the highest importance that the soul practice love very much in order that, being consumed rapidly, she may be scarcely retained here on earth but promptly reach the vision of her God face to face'" (CJ 7.27.5 [HLC, p. 113]).[95]

At the end of August, another statement that is crucial to our subject:

"Ah! it is incredible how all my hopes have been fulfilled. When I used to read St. John of the Cross, I begged God to work out in me what he wrote, that is, the same thing as though I were to live to be very old; to consume me rapidly in Love, and I have been answered!" (CJ 8.31.9 [HLC, p. 177]).

Such words, which show what goal Sr. Thérèse has reached, understanding herself to have attained the granting of her first request — to truly live the way of John of the Cross — can serve us as a makeshift conclusion. But these words are hardly surpassable.

* * *

---

[94] Cf. Appendices, pp. 156 ff.

[95] [The translation of Thérèse's given text (which differs in HLC [p. 113], LT 245 and P 12) is used throughout the present work in preference to that of St. John of the Cross's in K-RJ, p. 656: "It is vital for individuals to make acts of love in this life so that in being perfected in a short time, they may not be detained long, either here on earth or in the next life, before seeing God" — Trans.]

At the end of this historical and chronological chapter, we can already affirm that to reduce the influence of the Carmelite reformer to the adolescent years of Sr. Thérèse (age 17-18) does not correspond to reality. His presence indeed continues beyond that, even up to the final days of the saint of Lisieux.

In the following chapters we are going to show by means of a qualitative survey, to *what depth* his writings have penetrated the interior development of Sr. Thérèse of the Child Jesus and of the Holy Face.

2

THE SAINT OF LOVE

"He is the saint of Love par excellence."
(Sr. Thérèse to Sr. Marie of the Trinity)

"... these two doctors in the science of love..."
(Fr. Marie-Eugène of the Child Jesus,
Triduum of 1927)

The Saint of Love par excellence

IN A LATER TESTIMONY, WHICH CONFIRMS ALL OF the preceding ones, Sr. Marie of the Trinity in reference to her mistress of novices speaks of "This goal of love to which all her wishes aimed…"[1]

We have said that on her rather lonely path, the young Carmelite escaped the narrow atmosphere of her community by nourishing herself from the texts of John of the Cross that expanded her whole being, eager for the encounter with Jesus: "with *love* not only did I advance, I actually *flew* " (Ms A, p. 174 [80 v°]).

This is why we give a privileged place to Love, in the sense of divine *Agape*,[2] manifested among men by Jesus Christ and bestowed through Him on His disciples by the gift of the Holy Spirit.[3]

We are going to enumerate a dozen phrases of St. John of the Cross that profoundly affected Thérèse throughout her life. It is

---

[1] Letter of November 8, 1942 (VT 77, p. 50).

[2] [*Agape*, Greek for "love" in the sense of "pure self-gift" — Trans.]

[3] "In her writings, all the quotations that she takes from St. John of the Cross have but one goal: to highlight the unique value of love in order to attain to divine union" (P. Travert, *Études et Documents thérésiens* [Thérésian Studies and Documents], January 1935, p. 1).

difficult to establish a hierarchy or to find a progression among these imprints. As was always her habit, she thoroughly assimilated them with great liberty to nourish her own path.

* * *

I.   *It is, then, of the greatest importance that the soul exercise herself much in Love in order that, consuming herself rapidly, she hardly stops here below and arrives promptly in seeing her God Face to face.*[4]

This is an extremely important text that Thérèse quoted in a final image that she left to her sisters in June (?) 1897 (LT 245). She went back to it in *Her Last Conversations* in order to emphasize it: "With what longing and what consolation I repeated *from the beginning of my religious life* (emphasis mine) these (...) words of St. John of the Cross: 'It is of highest importance that the soul practice love very much in order that, being consumed rapidly, she may be scarcely retained here on earth but promptly reach the vision of her God face to face'" (CJ 7.27.5 [HLC, p. 113]). This means she had lived by these words for many years.

In this sentence, she expressed her life force, her desire to see face to Face. The same affirmation is to be found in the important *Consecration to the Holy Face* of August 6, 1896 (feast of the Transfiguration), which she made with two of her novices (Pri 12).

There is in Thérèse a certain haste, an impatience for the vision of God — "rapidly, promptly, hardly stopping here below" — that she felt like "a giant's course" (Ms A, p. 97 [44v°], quoting Ps 18:6). It is true that after a kind of slow preparation — those ten years from 1877 to the end of 1886, when she "turned in circles" — she launched into a race that never slackened but rather accelerated in the final two years of her life. At the age of 24, all would be

---

[4]   F, 1. 34 [K-RJ, p. 656].

finished; her life was "consummated," "worn out" (she often plays on the two words).[5] Her life is a shooting star that illumines the heavens with its light. She had never wished to die young, but she had the presentiment that she would depart quickly.[6] In fact, on September 30, 1897, everything was "accomplished."

Sr. Marie of the Trinity testified: "Certain passages of the works of our Father St. John of the Cross about love delighted her. She quoted them to me frequently, particularly this one: 'It is of the highest importance that the soul practice Love very much'...."[7]

Mother Agnès of Jesus testified that her sister "repeated several times in the infirmary this saying of St. John of the Cross."[8]

She certainly often associated this first text with a second.

II. The smallest movement of pure Love is more useful to the Church than all other works put together...[9]

In her *Consecration to the Holy Face* and in her testament she joined those two texts, which is very revealing. We can see in it her ultimate message.

On September 8, 1896, she had exclaimed: "O, my Jesus! I love You! I love the Church, my Mother! I recall that *the smallest act of PURE LOVE is of more value to her than all other works together.'* But is PURE LOVE in my heart? Are my measureless desires only but a dream, a folly?" (Ms B, p. 197 [4v°]).

The extraordinary fertility of Love is flowing from the heart of God, stimulating the extraordinary fertility of Thérèse's life. This has been verified since her death — it's necessary to say, rather, her "entering into Life" (LT 244) — since she finally (at the age of 23)

---

5 [In French there is a difference of only one letter: *consomée* and *consumée* — Trans.]

6 CJ 7.13.13 [HLC, p. 94].

7 VT 74, p. 151.

8 NPPA; cf. DE, p. 495 [HLC, p. 113].

9 C, 29. 2, introduction to stanza 29 [K-RJ, p. 587; cf. GC II, p. 1129 (LT 245)]. Thérèse's copy reads: "... is more profitable to the Church...."

found her true vocation in the Church and in the world: "O Jesus, my Love... my *vocation*, at last I have found it.... MY VOCATION IS LOVE!..." (Ms B, p. 194 [3v°]).

An unsurpassed cry, which in a certain way makes her Carmelite vocation "explode": to be "spouse, Carmelite and mother" was not enough for her any more. And certainly, wanting to be "Priest, Doctor, Soldier, Missionary, Martyr," she was not going to leave her monastery. But afterwards her life would take on a universal dimension, while her posthumous history is proof of the truth of her desires.

There is no grandiose self-exaltation in this young 24-year-old Carmelite who suffered from "infinite desires." She remained totally clear and remarked that "there is *no exaggeration* in [her] *little soul. Within it all is calm and at rest*" (Ms B, p. 189 [1v°]).

There is no doubt that Love coming from the heart of God — from the flesh of the Sacred Heart of the incarnate Son — animates the lives of all the saints. The special character of Thérèse does not lie in this, but in the fact that she situates herself in the heart of the Church with a universal perspective that embraces time and space "from the beginning of creation until the consummation of the ages" (Ms B, p. 193 [3r°]). Such an ambition could be taken as a piece of folly. Thérèse was very aware of that.[10] In fact this is reality, and again history has confirmed the truth of those desires that were not illusory but were put into her heart by the Holy Spirit.

On March 19, 1897, in a letter to Fr. Roulland, who was a missionary in China, she again took up the quoted text: "Saint John of the Cross has said: 'The smallest movement of pure love is more useful to the Church than all other works put together.' If it is so, how profitable for the Church must be your pains and trials, since it is for the love of Jesus alone that you suffer them *with joy*."[11] She underlined the two last words.

---

[10] "O my Jesus! What is your answer to all my follies?" (Ms B, p. 193 [3r°]).
[11] LT 221 [GC II, p. 1069].

*III.   In the evening of life, they will examine you on love. Learn then
to love God as He wills to be loved and forget yourself.*[12]

Taken from his book of *Maxims,* this maxim 70 caught
Thérèse's attention several times; it is the text she wrote on a holy
card of St. John of the Cross that she offered to Sr. Marie of the
Trinity on May 7, 1896.[13]

We have remarked that on the front of this image Sr. Thérèse
wrote, "*Through love,* to suffer and to be despised" — a truly characteristic addendum to the motto of St. John of the Cross that she
discovered in her youth. This "Through love," which dates from
1896, indicates the path she was to travel. Love had invaded everything since her discovery of Merciful Love and the Offering of June
9, 1895. Love is the fundamental reason for accepting suffering and
rules out all suspicion of drifting off course in whatever concerns
suffering.[14]

IV.   O Jesus, I know it, love is repaid by love alone.[15]

This is another motto that Sr. Thérèse made her own. She
wanted to work it into the coat of arms that she painted at the end
of her first manuscript (A), in a kind of banner below the two bla-
zons, that of Jesus (JHS) and that of Thérèse (FMT).[16]

But she had known this text for a long time, since she quoted
it already on March 12, 1889, in a letter to Céline: "Love is repaid

---

[12] Cf. *Sayings of Light and Love,* no. 60, K-RJ, p. 90.

[13] LT 188 (GC II, p. 953); reproduced in *Thérèse et Lisieux,* p. 173. On p. 170, there is the
image of John of the Cross offered to Thérèse by Mother Marie de Gonzague with the
same text.

[14] On this often heard objection, cf. A. Belford Ulanov, "Religious Devotion or Masoch-
ism? A psychoanalyst looks at Thérèse," in *Experiencing St. Thérèse Today,* ICS Publications, Washington, DC, 1990, pp. 140-156.

[15] Ms B, p. 195 (4r°), quoting C, 9. 7 (K-RJ, p. 506), commentary on stanza 9.

[16] [Cf. SS, pp. ii and 278 — Trans.]

by love alone"[17] and she added a passage of stanza 11 of the *Spiritual Canticle*: "the *wounds* of love are healed only by love."[18] This phrase is found again in her Manuscript B, p. 195 (4r°).

V.   *The affection [for the creature] is purely spiritual if the love of God grows when it grows, or if the love of God is remembered as often as the affection is remembered, or if the affection gives the soul a desire for God — if by growing in one, the soul grows also in the other.*[19]

These two further maxims of St. John of the Cross are found on the image given to Sr. Marie of the Trinity on May 7, 1896.

VI.   *He who walks in the love of God seeks... only to lose all things and himself for God...*[20]

is another maxim she cherished.

VII.   *At the end of her Manuscript A (1895) Thérèse wrote a splendid passage, which she supported with quotations from the Spiritual Canticle:*

"Neither do I desire any longer suffering or death, and still I love them both; it is *love* alone that attracts me, however. I desired them for a long time; I possessed suffering and believed I had touched

---

[17] LT 85 (GC I, p. 546). Drawn from the *Spiritual Canticle*, stanza 9. Cf. in a letter to Marie Guérin (LT 109, of 7/27-29/1890 [GC I, p. 641]: "the sickness of love is healed only through love!" Cf. our no. VIII, below.

[18] LT 85, *ibid.* [quoting CSB, sta. 11 (K-RJ, p. 514); see note 29 below — Trans.].

[19] Maxim 184 [in Thérèse's text. This is identified as maxim 129 in GC II, note 2, p. 953 — Trans.].

[20] Maxim 103. [The author, quoting Thérèse's text, has: "The one who truly loves God sees it as gain and reward to lose everything and to lose even oneself for God" — Trans.]

the shores of heaven, that the little flower would be gathered in the springtime of her life. Now, abandonment alone guides me. I have no other compass! I can no longer ask for anything with fervor except the accomplishment of God's will in my soul without any creature being able to set obstacles in the way. I can speak these words of the Spiritual Canticle of St. John of the Cross:

> *In the inner wine cellar I drank of my Beloved,*
> *and when I went abroad through all this valley*
> *I no longer knew anything,*
> *and lost the herd that I was following.*
> *Now I occupy my soul*
> *and all my energy in his service;*
> *I no longer tend the herd,*
> *nor have I any other work,*
> *now that my every act is LOVE!* [21]

"Or rather:

> *After I have known it*
> *LOVE works so in me*
> *that whether things go well or badly*
> *love turns them to one sweetness*
> *transforming the soul in ITSELF.* [22]

"How sweet is the way of *love*, dear Mother!" (Ms A, pp. 178-179, [83rº]).

Three quotations of the Spanish Carmelite are found within a few lines.

---

[21] Quoting C, stanzas 26 and 28 [K-RJ, p. 475; Thérèse emphasized the whole last line and capitalized the final word — Trans.]. This abandoning of the herd is to be found in the *Divin petit Mendiant de Noël* [Divine Little Christmas Beggar] (RP 5,26, of 12/25/ 1895, thus contemporaneous with this closing text of Ms A): "In order to delight the sweet Lamb / I no longer watch the flock...." Cf. PN 18.35 [*Poems*, p. 100]: "It's your love alone that transports me. / I leave my flock on the plain. / I don't take the trouble to tend it" [*Prayers*, p. 100].

[22] *A Gloss (with a spiritual meaning)*, st. 3 [K-RJ, p. 70; Thérèse capitalized the words — Trans.].

Obviously Thérèse could only have been intensely moved by this text which fulfilled her desire for intimate life with Jesus: "Now all my work is love." Is this not her entire life in Carmel?

In 1894 she quoted this text in a letter to Céline: "(Jesus) is pleased to see (Céline) in the desert, having no other duty but to love while suffering, without even *feeling* that she *loves*!..."[23]

We must go back to the sentence of John of the Cross about "Love works so in me / that whether things go well or badly / love turns them to one sweetness / transforming the soul in itself."[24] We have seen how this phrase was used in Manuscript A, p. 179 (83r°), and how Thérèse picked it up again in the poem offered to Sr. Marie of the Trinity for her profession on April 30, 1896. Here is the complete version:

> *Without support yet with support*
> *Living without Light, in darkness,*
> *I am wholly being consumed by Love....*

1 I have said an eternal goodbye
   To the world (what extreme happiness)!...
   ...Lifted higher than myself,
   I have no other Support than my God.
   And now I proclaim:
   What I value near Him
   Is to see and feel my soul
   Supported without any support!...

2 Though I suffer without Light
   In this life which lasts but a day,
   At least on earth I possess

---

[23] LT 157 [CG II, p. 841].

[24] *A Gloss (with a spiritual meaning)*, st. 3 [K-RJ, p. 70]. She repeats this in the image of the kaleidoscope: "Yes, to the extent that love is in our heart, when we don't move away from its center, *everything is well* and, as St. John of the Cross says: '*Love works so in me that whether things go well or badly, love turns them to one sweetness, transforming the soul in itself.*' The good Lord, looking at us through a little telescope, that is, as through himself, finds our miserable faults and our even more insignificant actions always beautiful. But, for that to happen, one mustn't move away from the little center! Because then, from thin scraps of wool and from tiny scraps of paper, behold what he will see" (MSG, p. 76).

The Heavenly life of Love....
In the way I have to walk,
Lies more than one danger,
But for Love I am willing to live
In exile's Shadows.

3   Love, I have experienced it,
Knows how to use (what power!)
The good and the bad it finds in me.
It transforms my soul into itself.
This Fire burning in my soul
Penetrates my heart forever.
Thus in its delightful flame
I am being wholly consumed by Love!...

(Pri 30)[25]

Thérèse copied his model yet still remained very personal. Her friends, listening to this poem as it was sung, were not aware that she had entered the trial of the darkness of faith since the beginning of April 1896. She was very much "without Light, in darkness...."

Concerning the Love that consumes her, it makes the most not only of the good that is in her but also of the *bad*. A daring thought, but profoundly Christian, an echo of which is found in the famous "*happy fault*" announced every year at the heart of the Paschal Vigil when the *Exultet* is chanted.[26] This is an essential affirmation of the victory of the Risen Lord and the concept of evil that denounces every temptation of Manichaeism.[27] There are not two Gods — one Good and one Evil — who wrestle in a doubtful combat. But faced with the Trinitarian God there is one creature, a spiritual rebel, who has lost his share since the death and resurrection of Jesus. The Fathers of the Church have always affirmed that

---

[25] *Prayers*, p. 148.

[26] ["O happy fault, that such a sin should merit such a redeemer!" — Trans.]

[27] [Manichaeism, religion founded by Mani (c.216-c.276), a visionary prophet, probably of Persian origin. Manichaeism synthesized elements from earlier religions and Christianity; it taught dualism between good and evil, the transmigration of souls, and the possibility of salvation. It lasted in the West into the 6th century — Trans.]

Satan, since that time, is only a raging chained dog that merely bites imprudent strays prowling near his corner.

It is true that Thérèse's demonology exists, but it is very discrete.[28] Her early experience had taught her that "a soul in the state of grace has nothing to fear from demons who are cowards, capable of fleeing before the gaze of a little child!" (Ms A, p. 28 [10vº]).

On July 6, 1893, in a significant letter to Céline, Thérèse already knew the text of St. John of the Cross: "Your Thérèse is not in the heights at this moment, but Jesus is teaching her 'to draw profit from everything, *from the good* and *the bad* she finds in herself'" (LT 142 [GC II, p. 795]).

VIII. *The sickness of love is healed only through love,*
writes St. John of the Cross.[29]

Thérèse quoted this saying in a letter to Céline of March 12, 1889: "Jesus' love for Céline can be understood only by Jesus!... Jesus has done foolish things for Céline.... Let Céline do *foolish things* for Jesus.... Love is repaid by love alone, and the *wounds* of love are healed only by love" (LT 85 [GC I, p. 546]).

The following year she repeated this quotation in a letter to Marie Guérin (July 27-29, 1890): "You are mistaken, my darling, if you believe that your little Thérèse walks always with fervor on the road of virtue. She is weak and very weak, and everyday she has a new experience of this weakness (...).

"Dear little Marie, as for myself, I know no other means of reaching perfection but (love).... Love, how well our heart is made for that!... Sometimes, I seek for another word to express love, but on this earth of exile words are powerless to express all the soul's vibrations, so we have to keep this one word: (love!)... Console Jesus,

---

[28] Cf. the appendix of *Triomphe de l'humilité* [Triumph of Humility], Cerf-DDB, 1975, pp. 128-133.

[29] CSB, sta. 11, pp. 200-202, according to the 1875 edition, translation of the Carmelites at Paris, used in *Letters* (cf. LT 109, note 5 [GC I, p. 643]); [cf. K-RJ, p. 473 — Trans.].

make Him *loved* by souls…. Jesus is sick, and we must state that *the sickness of love is healed only through love!…*" (LT 109 [GC I, p. 641] — we emphasize the last words).

Notice the liberty that Thérèse took in comparison with her Master: she modified the meaning by reversing the roles. According to the Spanish mystic, it is the soul that is sick with love and whose "sickness with love cannot be cured except by the presence and the figure of the object loved."[30] But for the Carmelite nun, it is Jesus who is sick, who is thirsty and hungry for his creature's love. This is completely the opposite! It must be said that John of the Cross himself gave a lot of freedom to his readers. He begins the *Spiritual Canticle* by affirming: "though we give some explanation of these stanzas, there is no reason to be bound to this explanation" (Prologue; cf. K-RJ, p. 470).

IX.   In the *Spiritual Canticle* B, a long passage captured Thérèse's attention:

"The power and the tenacity of Love is great, for love captures and binds God himself! Happy is the loving soul, since she possesses God for her prisoner, and he is surrendered to all her desires. God is such that those who act with love and friendship toward him will make him do all they desire, but if they act otherwise there is no speaking to him or power with him, even though they go to extremes. Yet by love they bind him with one hair. Knowing this, and knowing how far beyond her merits it was that he should have favored her with such sublime love and rich tokens of virtues and gifts, she attributes all to him in this stanza:

When you looked at me,
your eyes imprinted your grace in me;
for this you loved me ardently;

---

[30] CSB, 11.11; cf. note 29 above; [cf. K-RJ, p. 514 — Trans.].

and thus my eyes deserved
to adore what they beheld in you.[31]

Céline had copied the beginning of this passage into her Note-book.[32]

In a letter to Léonie of July 12, 1896, Thérèse spoke of "taking God by the Heart," of holding him back "by a hair": "I assure you that God is much better than you believe. He is content with a glance, a sigh of love.... As for me, I find perfection very easy to practice, because I have understood it is a matter of *taking hold of Jesus by His Heart....* Ah! we who are living in the law of love, how can we not profit by the loving advances our Spouse is making to us... how can we fear Him who allows Himself be enchained by *a hair* fluttering on our neck!... Let us understand, then, how to hold Him prisoner, this God who becomes the beggar of our love. When telling us that it is a hair that can effect this prodigy, He is showing us that the *smallest actions* done out of love are the ones which charm His Heart.... Ah! if we had to do great things, how much we would have to be pitied?... But how fortunate we are since Jesus allows Himself be enchained by the *smallest things...*" (LT 191 [GC II, pp. 965-966]).

The image of the hair that holds the fiancé captive obviously comes from the Song of Songs [4:9] according to the translation of the time. Jesus is a "beggar," Jesus is held "captive."[33]

Jesus, prisoner of our love — Thérèse found the beginning of the text of John of the Cross in the notebook of Céline that we already mentioned, under a slightly different form: "Great is the power and the authority of love since it seizes God. Happy the soul that loves because it holds God prisoner, submissive to what she wants!

---

[31] C, 32. 1 (cf. K-RJ, p. 599).

[32] VT 78, 1980, p. 160; cf. below and note 33. Cf. P. Descouvemont, *Thérèse de Lisieux et son prochain* [Thérèse of Lisieux and her neighbor], Lethielleux, 1962, p. 149, n. 142.

[33] Cf. LT 164 [GC II, p. 855]. The Songs of Songs is an essential source of John of the Cross (94 quotations) and of Thérèse (103 quotations). Cf. LT 191, of 7/12/96, to Léonie, where three of John of the Cross's themes are found.

Because such is the nature of God that when we accompany him on the way of love and goodness, we make him do what we wish."[34]

This being the case, it isn't astonishing to read in verse two of the famous song *Vivre d'Amour!* ["Living on Love!"], composed spontaneously on February 26, 1895:

> *The Spirit of Love sets me aflame with his fire.*
> *In loving you I attract the Father.*
> *My weak heart holds him forever*
> *O Trinity! You are Prisoner*
> *   Of my Love!...*   (PN 17.2)

Sometime later Thérèse wrote, at the request of Sr. Saint Vincent de Paul, a poem entitled *My Desires Near Jesus Hidden in His Prison of Love* (PN 25). The image of the "Divine Prisoner of the Tabernacle" was familiar to her,[35] but as we have mentioned, Thérèse emphasized the difference between God as prisoner *for* us (PN 25) and the Trinity as prisoner *in* us.[36]

X.   It is Love again that makes the maidens run. John of the Cross affirms:

Following your footprints / maidens run along the way.[37]

Obviously this is about Thérèse and Céline at Les Buissonets: "Jesus, wanting us to advance together, formed bonds in our hearts stronger than blood. He made us to become *spiritual sisters,*

---

[34] Note on C, stanza 32, according to the transcription Céline made of Msgr. Landriot's translation, p. 362. The beginning of this text is found again on the back of the image given to Sr. Marie of the Sacred Heart on 2/24/1896 (*Poésies* [Poems], vol. II, Cerf-DDB, 1979, p. 108; NEC, p. 350).

[35] For example, Ms A, p. 71 (31v°), p. 76 (34v°). Cf. image in P. Descouvemont-H.L. Loose, *Sainte Thérèse de Lisieux. La vie en images*, pp. 247-248.

[36] *Poetry*, note on verse 2 of PN 17, p. 87.

[37] C, sta. 25 [K-RJ, p. 475]. Text in Céline's Notebook, VT 78, p. 157.

and in us were realized the words of St. John of the Cross's Canticle (speaking to her Spouse, the bride exclaims):

> Following Your footprints
> Maidens run lightly along the way;
> The touch of a spark,
> The special wine,
> Cause flowings in them from the balsam of God.

"Yes, it was very *lightly* we followed in Jesus' footprints. The sparks of love He sowed so generously in our souls, and the delicious and strong wine He gave us to drink made all passing things disappear before our eyes, and from our lips came aspirations of love inspired only by Him" (Ms A, p. 103 [47vº/48rº]).

In *Living on Love* Thérèse evokes this lightness due to love:

> *Living on Love is giving without limit*
> *Without claiming any wages here below.*
> *Ah! I give without counting, truly sure*
> *That when one loves, one does not keep count!...*
> *Overflowing with tenderness, I have given everything,*
> *To his Divine Heart... lightly I run.*
> *I have nothing left but my only wealth:*
> *Living on Love.*   (PN 17.5)

XI.   In addition to these ten fundamental sayings about love taken from St. John of the Cross, we can add the long passage from Ezekiel 16 [vv. 6-13] that Thérèse quoted in her first manuscript.

Because the Bible was taken away from her in her novitiate, she could never have found this passage if she hadn't read it in the *Spiritual Canticle,* all the more so since the directness of the complete biblical text was off-putting to the novices. So in her manuscript (Ms A, pp. 101-102 [47rº]) Thérèse didn't hesitate applying to herself this narrative about a covenant of love:

"I was at the most dangerous age for young girls, but God did for me what Ezekiel reports in his prophecies: 'Passing by me, Jesus saw that the time had come for me to be loved. *He entered into a covenant with me and I became* His own. *He spread his mantle over me, he washed me with precious perfumes, He reclothed me in embroidered robes, He gave me priceless necklaces and ornaments. He nourished me with purest flour, with honey and oil in* abundance. *Then I became beautiful in His eyes and He made me a mighty queen!"*[38]

"Yes, Jesus did all this for me. I could take each word and prove it was realized in me" (Ms A, pp. 101-102 [47rº]).[39]

Rereading this passage of the *Spiritual Canticle* in the infirmary, the very sick patient circled with pencil the reference to Ezekiel 16.[40] One last time she reread in it her marvelous adventure of being the spouse of Jesus. A sign that the nearly unbearable sufferings of her illness, joined with the inner trial against faith, were not making her renounce her "engagement."[41]

XII. Finally it is necessary to emphasize the importance of the *Prayer of a Soul Taken with Love* by John of the Cross, which she read in his book of *Maxims*:[42]

Fr. Lucien Marie of Saint-Joseph wrote that "this prayer is a synthesis of the work of St. John of the Cross."[43]

Sr. Thérèse remembered especially the second part of it, about how grace works:

---

[38] [Cf. K-RJ, pp. 564-565 — Trans.]

[39] Cf. the introduction to *Répons de sainte Agnès* [The Responses of Saint Agnes] (PN 26, 1/21/1896), *Poetry*, p. 136.

[40] Page 335 in the version Thérèse read.

[41] Cf. introduction to PN 26 (*Poetry*, p. 136).

[42] Pp. 103-106 (K-RJ, pp. 87-88).

[43] *Du désespoir à l'action de grâce*, *Revue thomiste* [From despair to giving thanks, Thomistic Revue] April-September 1971, p. 288.

"Mine are the heavens and mine is the earth. Mine are the na-
tions, the just are mine, and mine the sinners. The Angels are mine,
and the Mother of God, and all things are mine; and God himself
is mine and for me, because Christ is mine and all for me. What
do you ask, then, and seek, my soul? Yours is all of this, and all is
for you. Do not engage yourself in something less…" [K-RJ, pp.
87-88.]

References to this text are numerous. As early as August 15,
1892, she wrote to Céline who was at the Musse: "Céline, the vast
solitudes, the enchanting horizons opening up before you must be
speaking volumes to your soul? I myself see nothing of all that, but
I say with Saint John of the Cross, 'My Beloved is the mountains,
the lonely, wooded valleys, etc.'" (LT 135 [GC II, p. 752], quoting
C, stanza 14).[44]

In a letter to Céline of October 19, 1892: "Like Zachaeus, we
climbed a tree to see Jesus…. Then we could say with Saint John of
the Cross: 'All is mine, all is for me, the earth is mine, the heavens
are mine, God is mine, and the Mother of my God is mine'" (LT
137 [GC II, p. 761]).

In the very long letter of February 23, 1896, for her sister's
profession, Thérèse came back to this quotation: "All is *ours*, all is
for us, for in Jesus we have all!…" (LT 182 [GC II, p. 930]).

Sr. Geneviève emphasized that this prayer of St. John of the
Cross "filled [her sister] with joy and hope," expressing for her "that
admirable Communion of Saints which was her delight."[45]

Thérèse's sister didn't forget the *Canticle of Céline*, based prin-
cipally on the *Prayer of a Soul Taken with Love*, which copies the
format of: "In You… I have…"[46]:

---

[44] ["My Beloved, the mountains, / and lonely wooded valleys" (K-RJ, p. 473) — Trans.]
[45] DE/G in DE, p. 615; [cf. LT 182, note 23 (GC II, p. 932) — Trans.].
[46] PN 18, stanzas 36, 38, 39, etc. [*Poetry*, p. 100]. In PN 18A, *Qui a Jésus a tout* [He who
Has Jesus Has Everything], synthesizing PN 18, the epigraph is this: "Several thoughts
are taken from the *Spiritual Canticle* of St. John of the Cross."

In you, I have everything, the earth and even Heaven.
The Flower that I pick, O my King,
Is you!...   [PN 18.36]

An influence from the *Spiritual Canticle B* is noticeable
throughout the stanzas; for example:

> I've the beautiful lake, I've the valley
> Lonely and all wooded.   (sta. 46)
> > *I have, in my Beloved,*
> > *The lonely wooded valleys*
> > > (CSB, sta. 14; p. 229)[47]

> I've the melodious lyre,
> Sounding solitude   (sta. 40)
> > *silent music*
> > *sounding solitude*
> > > (CSB, sta. 15; p. 229)[48]

> Night like the sunrise   (sta. 42)
> > *the tranquil night*
> > *at the time of the rising dawn*
> > > (CSB, sta. 15)[49]

Thérèse's second theater play about Joan of Arc ends on a song
alternating between Joan and the saints: "It's my turn. — *It's your*
turn. — Oh! what extraordinary happiness. All of heaven belongs
to me. — *All of heaven is yours.* — The angels and the Saints!...
Mary!... My God himself. They are mine.
    They belong to you."[50]
    In her canticle, *To My Little Brothers in Heaven,* Thérèse sees

---

47 [Cf. K-RJ, p. 473 and note 42 above — Trans.]
48 [Cf. K-RJ, p. 473 — Trans.]
49 [*Idem.* — Trans.]
50 RP 3, 23v°. *Théâtre au Carmel* [Theater at Carmel], Cerf-DDB, 1985, p. 157; Œ/T, p. 857.

the Holy Innocents in Paradise approaching: "The treasures of the Elect, their palms, their crowns, / All is yours" (PN 44.5).[51]

Also in her long poem about the Virgin Mary, she sees herself sharing her Mother's virtues and love:

The treasures of a mother belong to her child,
And I am your child, O my dearest Mother.
Aren't your virtues and your love mine too?[52]

Sr. Thérèse had also read in the *Spiritual Canticle*:
"... the soul easily extracts the sweetness of love from all the things that happen to her.... Thus everything leads her to love. And being informed and fortified as she is with love, she neither feels nor tastes nor knows the things that happen to her, whether delightful or bitter, since as we said the soul knows nothing else but love."[53]

In the poem entitled *The Queen of Heaven to Her Beloved Child Marie of the Holy Face,* Thérèse wrote:

Don't worry, Marie,
About each day's duties.
For your task in this life
Must only be: "Love!"

But if someone comes to find fault
That your works cannot be seen,
You can say, "I love much,
That is my wealth here below!..."[54]

St. John of the Cross liked to insist on the "resemblance obtained through union in love" between the lover and the loved one. This he did in the explanations of stanzas 12 and 32 of the *Spiritual*

---

[51] [*Poetry*, p. 182 — Trans.]

[52] [PN 54, *Pourquoi je t'aime, ô Marie,* (Why I Love You, O Mary), sta. 5; *Poetry*, p. 216 — Trans.]

[53] C, 27. 8; cf. K-RJ, p. 583.

[54] PN 13.15-16 [*Poetry*, p. 78].

Canticle that Thérèse loved to comment on herself for Sr. Marie of the Trinity: "By the eyes of the Bridegroom [the soul] refers to God's mercy: He descends in mercy on the soul, impressing and infusing his love and grace in her, making her beautiful and lifting her so high as to make her a partaker in his very divinity...."[55]

Thérèse brought up this fundamental objective of the union of love. We are called to be God through participation in the Son, through the Spirit. Very early, in a beautiful passionate letter of March 12, 1889, she wrote to Céline: "Life is passing away.... Eternity is advancing in great strides.... Soon we shall live the very life of Jesus.... After having drunk at the fountain of all sorrows, we shall be deified at the very fountain of all joys, all delights. (...) Jesus' love for Céline can be understood only by Jesus!"[56]

"We are greater than the whole universe, and one day *we ourselves* shall have a divine existence...."[57]

"What a mystery is our grandeur in Jesus."[58]

This refers to the great theme of adoptive participation in the Love of God, a subject also of *The Living Flame of Love* whose last stage reaches the heights of spiritual marriage (end of the third stanza). John of the Cross arrives at participation in the spiration[59] of love in the Trinity (fourth stanza): "It is a spiration that God produces in the soul, in which, by that awakening of lofty knowledge of the Godhead, he breathes the Holy Spirit in it in the same proportion as its knowledge and understanding of him, absorbing it most profoundly in the Holy Spirit, rousing its love with a divine exquisite quality and delicacy according to what it beholds in him. Since the breathing is filled with good and glory, the Holy Spirit, through

---

[55] C, 32.4; cf. K-RJ, p. 600.

[56] LT 85 [GC I, p. 546]. Cf. RP 2, 8rº: "Also in the Holy Homeland / My chosen ones will be glorious / In their partaking of my life / I will make them gods also!..."

[57] LT 83 [GC I, p. 542].

[58] LT 137 [GC II, p. 761].

[59] ["Spiration" is the theological term for the Trinitarian action of mutual, complementary Love between the Father and the Son, namely the Holy Spirit; applied to the soul, it is the indwelling of this Trinitarian Love — Trans.]

this breathing, filled the soul with good and glory in which he enkindled in it love of himself, indescribably and incomprehensibly,
in the depths of God...."[60]

In Thérèse's Manuscript B, the little bird enters the furnace
of the Holy Trinity by means of the eagle that carries it on its back.[61]
Here we are in line with deification according to the Greek Fathers,
and with communion according to the Last Supper Discourse in John
17.

Now, St. John of the Cross quotes the priestly prayer in the
explanation of stanzas 36 and 39 of the *Spiritual Canticle*.[62] It is the
same text Thérèse quoted at the end of her manuscript C[63] in order
to express her union with Christ. She justified her boldness (putting St. John's text into the feminine in order to adapt it to herself)
because everything is communion between the Son and the disciple.
She relies on John 17:10: *"all things that are mine are yours, and yours
are mine"* [quoted from Ms C, p. 255 (34r°)]. Is this meeting just a
coincidence? Whatever it may be, John of the Cross and Thérèse
have arrived at the same summit: the ultimate message of Christ just
before his Passion.

* * *

We notice again the liberty of interpretation Thérèse took with
the Spanish saint.

In the infirmary, she spoke about her poverty to Mother Agnès
of Jesus:

"I can depend on nothing, on no good works of my own in
order to have confidence. For example, I'd like to be able to say that
I've carried out all my obligations of reciting my prayers for the dead.

---

[60] F, 4. 16 (K-RJ, p. 715).

[61] Ms B, p. 200 (5v°); cf. Fr. Marie-Eugène of the Child Jesus, *Je veux voir Dieu* [I want to
see God], p. 1031; read C, 31.8 [K-RJ, p. 598]; Dt 32:11; Ex 19:4.

[62] Book II, pp. 64 and 99-100 in Thérèse's copy; cf. K-RJ, pp. 612.

[63] [Ms C, p. 255ff. (34r°-35v°) — Trans.]

This poverty, however, was a real light and a grace for me. I was thinking that never in my life would I be able to pay my debts to God; this was real riches, real strength for me, if I wanted to take it in this way. Then I made this prayer to God: O my God, I beg You, pay the debt that I have acquired with regard to the souls in purgatory, but do it as God, so that it be infinitely better than if I had said my Offices for the Dead. And then I remembered with great consolation these words of St. John of the Cross' canticle: 'Pay all debts.' I had always applied this to Love. I felt this grace can't be expressed in words; it's far too sweet! We experience such great peace when we're so totally poor, when we depend upon no one except God."[64]

As Fr. E. Renault has remarked: "She understands this passage as the soul's plea that God remit the obligations she has not fulfilled, whereas John of the Cross was hearing the soul singing about the happiness of *being recompensed by sweet consolations for all she had suffered*."[65]

* * *

At the end of this chapter, we note that the saying reported by Sr. Marie of the Trinity is perfectly verified. On her solitary way, Sr. Thérèse of the Child Jesus and the Holy Face truly encountered "the Saint of Love par excellence." This encounter was certain within the intuitions of the novice who was still shy and taken aback by her fellow sisters. But after 1891 she dared to go forward with audacity, "on the waves of confidence and love," which opened her to the light of the way of spiritual childhood three years later.

The contribution of the mystical Doctor was decisive — and explicit — on the journey of the young Carmelite of Lisieux.

"What she found in the *Living Flame* and the *Spiritual Canticle* were limitless horizons, the horizons of the love belonging to

---

[64] CJ 8.6.4 [HLC, p. 137], quoting VFA, 2.6, p. 183 of Thérèse's copy [cf. F, sta. 2, v. 5 in K-RJ, p. 640].

[65] *Carmel* magazine, 1990/3, p. 24.

Trinitarian life. This reading revealed to her the presence of God that the preachers of her time did not tell her about, but made her especially practice asceticism. In John of the Cross she found an asceticism of another kind, and greater, more profound truths. She attached herself to St. John of the Cross and learned him by heart."[66]

---

[66] Fr. Marie-Eugène of the Child Jesus, *Retraite sacerdotale* [Priestly Retreat], 1957, p. 102.

3

"THIS MASTER OF FAITH"

> *"Thérèse, if you look at her really well, was above all a hero of faith."*
>
> (Stanislas Fumet, *Mikael*, p. 183)

> *"Supported without any support…"*
>
> (PN 30)

O<small>N</small> N<small>OVEMBER</small> 4, 1984 P<small>OPE</small> J<small>OHN</small> P<small>AUL</small> II re-minded people in Segovia that he had written his thesis on *faith according to St. John of the Cross*,[1] "this master of faith," as the Pope called him.

In the writings of Thérèse of Lisieux, there are fewer references about faith taken from John of the Cross than there are about Love.

The Spanish master's essential teaching on faith is found in his *Ascent of Mount Carmel*, Book II, with its 32 chapters. Other texts can be read in *The Dark Night*, Book II. But it must be said again, we don't know whether Sr. Thérèse really read these books. She kept almost nothing of the theological expression of faith taught by the Saint, but she held onto her little book of his *Maxims*.[2] We know that she read and reread this one. The chapter on *Faith* contains Maxims 17-36. It is a veritable little treatise on this theological vir-

---

[1] Published by Éditions du Cerf in 1980, 224 pages [also in English by Ignatius Press — Trans.].

[2] [This anthology with its proper numbering exists only in the French; it can be found in the Archives of the Lisieux Carmel — Trans.]

tue. It is best to reproduce the maxims here, since these are the ones the young Carmelite meditated on.

In the epigraph there are two sayings from Scripture: "I will betroth you to me in faith" (Ho 2:21) and "Without faith, it is impossible to please God. Whoever would approach union with God should believe in His existence…" (Heb 11:6).[3]

17   The road of faith is the only good and sure way. Souls who want to advance in virtue must walk on it, shutting their eyes to everything that comes from the senses or from one's own thought, however enlightened it may be. [Cf. A, II. 1 (K-RJ, p. 155).]

18   When inspirations come from God, they are always regulated by patterns of God's law or of faith, and it is through perfection of faith that the soul always draws closer to God.

19   The soul that faithfully adheres to the insights and truths of faith walks safely without any danger of going astray, because it can be taken as a common rule that a soul goes astray only when it follows its own inclinations, tastes, reasons and ideas. These almost always make the soul commit sin, either through excess or failure, inclining it towards what isn't the right thing to do at all in God's service.

20   With faith, the soul walks without having to fear the devil, its strongest and shrewdest enemy. Even St. Peter did not find stronger means to help against the devil, and said to the believers: "Resist him by the firmness of your faith" [1 Pet 5:9].

21   In order for a soul to approach God and unite with Him, it is better to advance without understanding than with understanding, and in a total forgetfulness of creatures, exchanging whatever is comprehensible and changeable in creatures for what is never-changing and incomprehensible, God Himself.

22   Light is useful for us in this visible world to keep us from falling. But in the things of God, on the contrary, it is better not to see; and the soul thus finds more security.

---

[3]   [Cf. A, II. 4 (K-RJ, p. 160) — Trans.]

23 Since it is certain that in this life we will know God more through what He is not than through what He is, the soul must move towards Him by rejecting all perception as much as possible, natural or supernatural.

24 No perception or thought about supernatural things will help us as much to grow in divine love as the least act of living faith and hope in God, completely devoid of all light.

25 At the same time, no creature knows how to evolve into a new form by following the laws of natural generation without losing the one it had before. It is likewise necessary to destroy the animalistic life and sensory life in our soul, in order to give place to the pure life of the spirit.

26 Do not look for the presence of creatures when you want to keep the features of the Divine Face clear and pure in your soul. But rid and clear your mind of every created object. Thus you will walk among the lights of God, who does not resemble the creature.

27 Faith is the surest refuge for the soul; and the Holy Spirit Himself is then its light. Because the more pure and rich a soul is in the perfections of a living faith, the more it abundantly possesses charity infused by God; the more it receives enlightenment and supernatural gifts.

28 One of the most remarkable favors that the Lord gives to a soul during this life — again, not lasting, but transient — is to grant it such a clear knowledge and such a heightened feeling of His divinity, that it understands and sees very clearly that it is impossible to have full understanding and feeling here below.

29 When a soul holds onto its own knowledge or onto its tastes and feelings in order to reach God, not seeing that these same means are without any value and proportion for such a goal, it easily gets lost or stops en route, failing to attach itself blindly to faith alone that is its true guide.

30 It is a surprising thing that happens nowadays. When a soul is using the Four Last Things[4] to consider divine things, and

---

[4] [Death, Judgment, Heaven and Hell — Trans.]

hears within itself the sound of some inner word, in a moment of stillness it takes this as something sacred or divine, without the slightest doubt in the world. "God," it says, "has spoken to me," "God has answered me." Now this is not true. It is the soul itself speaking to itself and answering itself, by the very fact of its own desire.

31   Whoever in our day wants to ask for visions or revelations seems to me to offend the Lord by not keeping his eyes solely on his Anointed One. And God would have the right to answer him, "Behold, you have my beloved Son, in whom I am well pleased. Listen to him and do not look for new ways of teachings. For in him and through him I have spoken to you and have revealed everything you could desire and ask for. I gave him to you as your brother, master, friend, ransom, and for your reward."

32   We have to let ourselves be guided in everything by the doctrine of Jesus Christ and his Church, seeking therein the remedy for all our ignorance and spiritual weakness. For it is there, in fact, that we will find an ever-effective and ever-available remedy for all our offenses. Whoever strays from this way will be culpable not only of vain curiosity but also of insupportable recklessness.

33   One should not believe or accept anything by supernatural communication than what agrees with the doctrine of Jesus Christ and the word of his ministers.

34   The soul that wants to have revelations commits at least a venial sin; and those who urge the soul towards this desire or consent to it, are likewise sinning even if they mean it for a good purpose, because there is no need whatsoever for any of that. Natural reason and the doctrine of the gospel are sufficient to guide us in everything.

35   The soul that desires revelations diminishes so much the perfection it has already acquired, by not letting itself be guided by faith alone. And it also opens the door for the devil, inviting him to deceive it by other, very similar revelations, which he knows how to wonderfully disguise and make appear equally good.

36   All the wisdom of the saints consists in knowing how to strongly direct their will towards God, accomplishing His holy law and divine counsels perfectly.

Moreover, if Thérèse had attentively read stanza 12 of the *Spiritual Canticle B*, explanation 2-6 [K-RJ, pp. 516-517], she could have found there another substantial summary on faith.

Although all of this could have been thoroughly assimilated by Sr. Thérèse, she has particularly integrated it in a vital manner. In her writings there are few quotations about the virtue of faith, but there is a spiritual attitude that shows her habitually living in faith throughout her Carmelite life.[5]

This is what Sr. Geneviève (Céline) testifies: "(Thérèse) lived on bare faith her entire life. There was no soul less consoled in prayer. She confided to me that she spent seven years in totally arid prayer; her annual and monthly retreats were torture for her. Nonetheless, people believed she was flooded with spiritual consolations, so unctuous were her words and deeds, so intimately was she united to God."[6]

Concerning Sr. Thérèse's difficulties during her retreats, we have already quoted the testimony of Mother Agnès of Jesus: "She suffered a lot during the conferences when it was said how easy it is to fall into mortal sin, even by a simple thought. To her it seemed so difficult to offend God, when one loves him! During the whole time of those exercises, I saw her pale and haggard, she could no longer eat or sleep and would have become sick if that would have gone on."[7]

Thérèse herself confirms this: "Ordinarily, the retreats that are preached are more painful to me than the ones I make alone" (Ms A, p. 173 [80r°]). She experienced aridity in prayer very early on.

---

[5]   In the Manuscripts, the word *faith* is found 24 times; in the *Letters*, seven times; in her other writings, 57 times. The word *love* appears 756 times in her writings.

[6]   MSG, p. 103.

[7]   PA, p. 467.

We have echoes of it in the 14 little notes written during her four-day retreat for her reception of the habit, January 5-10, 1889.

Jesus tells her absolutely nothing

The 16-year-old novice: "Nothing, near Jesus. Aridity!... Sleep!... (...) I am, however, VERY *happy*, happy to suffer what Jesus wants me to suffer. [...] Since Jesus wants to sleep why will I hinder him? I am only too happy that He doesn't bother with me, for He is showing me that I am not a stranger when treating me this way, for, I assure you, He is going to no trouble about carrying on a conversation with me!..."[8]

To Sr. Marie of the Sacred Heart (her sister Marie): "The poor little lamb (Thérèse herself) can say nothing to Jesus, and, above all, Jesus says absolutely nothing to it; pray for it so that its retreat be pleasing just the same to the Heart of Him who ALONE reads into the depths of the soul!... (...) This [...] suffering is known to Jesus alone!..."[9]

To Sr. Agnès of Jesus: "my Fiancé (Jesus) (...) prefers leaving me in darkness to giving me a false light which would not be *Himself*!... (...) He alone is perfect joy, when he appears to be absent!... Today more than yesterday, if that were possible, I was deprived of all consolation. I thank Jesus, who finds this good for my soul, and that, perhaps if He were to console me, I would stop at this sweetness; but He wants that *all* be for *Himself*!... (...) Although Jesus is giving me no consolation, He is giving me a peace so great that it is doing me more good!..."[10]

Again to Sr. Agnès: "The lamb (Agnès)[11] is mistaken in believing that Jesus' toy is not in darkness; it is immersed in darkness.

---

[8] LT 74 [GC I, pp. 499-500], to Sr. Agnès of Jesus.

[9] LT 75 [GC I, p. 501].

[10] LT 76 [GC I, p. 504].

[11] ["Agneau" and "Agnus" mean "lamb" in French and Latin respectively. "Agnus"/"Agnès" is a delightful play on words that is characteristic of Thérèse's merry imagination — Trans.]

Perhaps, and the little lamb agrees with this, this darkness is light, but in spite of everything it is darkness.... Its *only* consolation is a strength and a very great peace, and, then, it wants to be as Jesus wills it to be; that is its joy, otherwise, all is sadness.... (...) I believe that the work of Jesus during this retreat has been to detach me from all that is not Himself.... If you only knew how great my joy is not to have anything with which to please Jesus!... It is a refined joy (but in no way felt)."[12]

Several months later, from August 28 to September 7, 1890 (she is 17 and a half), she made a new retreat before her profession. We have some notes from that period (LT 110 and LT 117), but this time a few lines from the first manuscript give us more precise information: "the retreat preceding my Profession (...) was far from bringing me any consolations since the most absolute aridity and almost total abandonment were my lot. Jesus was sleeping as usual in my little boat" (Ms A, p. 165 [75v°]). Further on, she continues: "Just as *all those that followed it*, my Profession retreat was one of great aridity" (Ms A, p. 165 [76r°] — emphasis mine).

Let us now read some extracts from the pencil-written notes during this retreat.

The young novice speaks about her journey that runs through "a subterranean passage where it is neither cold nor hot, where the sun does not shine, and in which the rain or the wind does not visit, a subterranean passage where I see nothing but a half-veiled light, the light which was diffused by the lowered eyes of my Fiancé's Face!... My Fiancé says nothing to me, and I say nothing to Him either except that *I love Him more than myself*, and I feel at the bottom of my heart that it is true, for I am more His than my own!... I don't see that we are advancing towards the summit of the mountain since our journey is being made underground, but it seems to me that we are approaching it without knowing how. The route on

---

[12] LT 78 [GC I, p. 511]. Fr. Pichon will write to her on 3/27/1890 from Montreal: "your thanks must be multiplied on the nights of days of aridity and bitterness" (LC 126 [GC I, p. 608]).

which I am has no consolation for me, and nevertheless it brings me all consolations since Jesus is the one who chose it, and I want to console Him alone, alone!..."[13] "Subterranean" and "underground" clearly evoke night.

She will explain the image in a letter to Sr. Marie of the Sacred Heart: "I assure you that she (Thérèse) hardly hears the heavenly harmonies. Her wedding trip is very arid; it is true, her Fiancé is having her travel through fertile and magnificent countries but the *night* prevents her from admiring anything and, especially, from enjoying these marvels. You're going to believe that she's saddened by this, but no, on the contrary, she is happy to follow her Fiancé because of her love for *Himself alone* and not because of His gifts... He alone is so beautiful, so ravishing!... even when He is *silent*... even when He *hides Himself*!..."[14]

To Sr. Agnès of Jesus on Monday, September 1st: "But I don't understand the retreat I am making; I think of nothing; in a word, I am in a very dark subterranean passage!... Oh! ask Jesus, you who are my light, that He not permit souls to be deprived of lights that they need because of me, but that my darkness may serve to enlighten them...."[15]

A sentence of capital importance at which we have to pause, because it brings up what Thérèse would write at the end of her life, in her great trial of faith and hope that lasted 18 months. She begged God for "her unbelieving brothers" to have light and accepts on their account to remain "alone" in darkness. "May all those who were not enlightened by the bright flame of faith one day see it shine" (Ms C, p. 212 [6r°]).

Thus the novice already realized that her nocturnal trial was co-redemptive, missionary. There is a difference, however, between the two nights[16]: the first one is purifying (and already co-redemp-

---

[13] LT 110 [GC I, p. 652], to Sr. Agnès of Jesus.

[14] LT 111 [GC I, pp. 654-655].

[15] LT 112 [GC I, p. 658].

[16] Notice that the vocabulary of 1890 is close to that of 1897: "subterranean passage" (1890), "dark tunnel" (1897).

tive, because it isn't necessary to wait to be totally purified in order to participate in redemption);[17] the second one is essentially co-re-demptive, even if some traces of purification remain.[18]

It is truly astonishing that such a young religious understood this connection between her darkness and its salvific repercussion on "unbelievers." It would take all her strength to hold onto this communion of saints seven years later, in the final months of her life.

Let us finish reading letter 112: "Ask Him, too, that I make a good retreat and that He may be as pleased as He can be; then I, too, will be pleased, and I will consent, if this be His will, to walk all my life on the dark road on which I am, provided that one day I reach the summit of the mountain of Love.[19] But I believe this will not be here below."[20]

Another astounding declaration of such a young Carmelite's respect for this life of dark faith, which she accepts until death, as long as the Beloved's will be done. Notice that she will have the same disposition in 1895: "Jesus… will undoubtedly awaken before my great eternal retreat, but instead of being troubled about it this only gives me extreme pleasure" (Ms A, p. 165 [75v°]). Let us measure the strength of those words.

We find the same vocabulary three days later, September 4, 1890, in a note to Sr. Agnès of Jesus: "My soul is always in the sub-terranean passage, but it is *very happy*, yes, happy to have no conso-lation whatsoever, for I find that then its love is not like the love of earthly fiancées who are always looking at the hands of their fiancés to see if they have brought them any gifts, or else at their faces to catch there a smile of love which delights them…."[21]

---

[17] Fr. Marie-Eugène of the Child Jesus, *Je veux Dieu* [I want to see God], p. 817, n. 1.

[18] "Now (this ordeal) is taking away everything that could be a natural satisfaction in my desire for heaven" (Ms C, p. 214 [7v°]).

[19] Reminiscent of St. John of the Cross's *Ascent of Mount Carmel*. Cf. LT 105; LT 112; Ms B, p. 188 (1v°), etc.

[20] [LT 112 (GC I, p. 658) — Trans.]

[21] [LT 115 (GC I, p. 667) — Trans.]

And on Monday, September 8, 1890, Sr. Thérèse of the Child Jesus made her profession, "flooded by a river of peace," "and it was in this peace 'which surpasses all understanding'" (Ph 4:7) that she made her final vows (Ms A, p. 166 [76vº]).

She has attained a new dimension. She was already in the darkness of this "peace" that inundated her. She was already living in what we would spontaneously call a paradox, but which Fr. Marie-Eugène of the Child Jesus calls "antinomy,"[22] to know the coexistence in the soul of two apparently opposed feelings: joy/suffering, obscurity/peace, dryness/serenity....[23]

We already know that at the time of her clothing, she filled out the rest of her religious name: *of the Holy Face*. From her profession on, she started to sign her name as Sr. Thérèse of the Child Jesus and *of the Holy Face*,[24] for in her wedding announcement, the "dowry" of her Divine Spouse is "The Childhood of Jesus and His Passion."[25]

It shows us the echo in her heart of her father's illness, the trial that pierced her most profoundly ever since Louis Martin was hospitalized at the Bon Saveur in Caen (February 12, 1889), but also her austere regimen of bare faith in prayer. She began reading the "Doctor of Faith" and already profoundly lives his teaching on "faith, the way of prayer."[26]

---

[22] [A philosophical/theological term for two laws that oppose each other, coexisting in a contradictory state — Trans.]

[23] *Je veux voir Dieu* [I want to see God], list with analytics, p. 1083: the word *antinomy*. Cf. *Au souffle de l'Esprit* [By inspiration of the Spirit], published by Carmel, 1990, pp. 127, 179-180. Eng. tr. *Where the Spirit Breathes*, Alba House, 1998.

[24] Cf. LT 80 and LT 119 [GC I, pp. 520 and 682], to Sr. Martha of Jesus.

[25] LT 118 [GC I, p. 679] and Ms A, p. 168 [77vº].

[26] Title of an article by Fr. F. Retoré in *Communio*, num. X:4, July-August 1985, pp. 1-14.

Prayer: The sleep of Thérèse and the sleep of Jesus

Prayer for Sr. Thérèse continued to be this path of dryness and aridity in which the theological virtue of Faith was her light in the darkness. She mentions this dryness quite often in her notes: "[Spiritual] aridity was my daily bread" (Ms A, p. 157 [73vº]). "Sometimes a word comes to console me [...] at the end of prayer (after having remained in silence and aridity)" (Ms B, p. 187 [1rº]). "Sometimes when my mind is in such great aridity that it is impossible to draw forth one single thought to unite me to God, I *very slowly* recite an 'Our Father' and then the angelic salutation" (Ms C, p. 243 [25vº]).

On July 18, 1893, she wrote to Céline concerning the darkness and dryness: "when I *am feeling* nothing, when I am INCAPABLE *of praying....*"[27] But if Jesus is asleep within her,[28] we have to say that Thérèse also falls asleep at prayer time and during the thanksgiving after Communion. In hindsight, this passage in manuscript A is not insignificant: "Really, I am far from being a saint, and what I have just said is proof of this; instead of rejoicing, for example, at my aridity, I should attribute it to my little fervor and lack of fidelity; I should be desolate for having slept (for seven years) during my hours of prayer and my *thanksgivings...*" (Ms A, p. 165 [75vº]).

Sr. Marie of the Trinity, who entered the Carmel in Lisieux on June 16, 1894, only three years before the death of her novice mistress, could testify to the persistence of this sleepiness in her life. "She was clinging to her seat, she was falling forward during Mass. She fell from tiredness. She was sleeping almost all the time during her thanksgivings, on her knees, head to the floor. She couldn't prevent it."[29]

---

[27] LT 143 [GC II, p. 801].

[28] Cf. LT 144 160, 165 [GC II, pp. 804, 849, 862]. Cf. *Living on Love*: "Living on Love, when Jesus is sleeping / Is rest on stormy seas. / Oh! Lord, don't fear that I'll wake you. / I'm waiting in peace for Heaven's shore...." (PN 17.9 [*Poetry*, p. 91]). Cf. PN 13.14 [p. 78]; PN 24.32 [p. 131]; PN 42.1-4 [p. 175].

[29] Notes made by Fr. Philippe de la Trinité, OCD, after a parlor visit with Sr. Marie of the Trinity in 1940. Cf. *Thérèse de Lisieux, la sainte de l'enfance spirituelle* [Thérèse of Lisieux, the saint of spiritual childhood], Lethielleux, 1980, note 4.

Describing her actual life in the parable of the little bird (Ms B of September 1896), Thérèse doesn't omit speaking about her tiredness during prayer: "Yes, this is still one of the weaknesses of the little bird: when it wants to fix its gaze upon the Divine Sun, and when the clouds prevent it from seeing a single ray of that Sun, in spite of itself, its little eyes close, its little head is hidden beneath its wing, and the poor little thing falls asleep, believing all the time that it is fixing its gaze upon its Dear Star. When it awakens, it doesn't feel desolate; its little heart is at peace and it begins once again its work of *love*" ([p. 199] 5r°).

No Consolation

A lot of courage and faith are necessary to renounce all consolation when you commit yourself to the way of prayer. "I can't say that I frequently received consolations when making my thanksgivings after Mass; perhaps it is the time when I receive the least. However, I find this very understandable, since I have offered myself to Jesus not as one desirous of her own consolation in His visit but simply to please Him who is giving Himself to me" (Ms A, p. 172 [79v°]).

She wrote to her cousin Marie Guérin: "Don't be troubled about feeling no consolation in your Communions; this is a trial that you must bear with love."[30]

She wrote to Céline in 1890: "Let us detach ourselves from the *consolations* of Jesus in order to attach ourselves to *Him*!..."[31]

When Léonie Martin left the monastery of the Visitation in Caen yet another time on July 20, 1895, her sister Thérèse wrote to her Aunt Guérin: "God, who willed to try our faith, was sending us no consolation whatever...."[32]

---

[30] LT 93 [GC I, p. 576].

[31] LT 105 [GC I, p. 618].

[32] LT 178 [GC II, p. 908].

The following year, a sentence in manuscript B pulls every-thing together: "Do not believe that I am swimming in consolations; oh no, my consolation is to have none on earth" (p. 187 [1r°]). Her sister Marie of the Sacred Heart, who received this letter, is evidently unaware that Thérèse has been undergoing the trial of faith since Easter of 1896.

In a life consecrated to prayer, these habitual states of aridity and dryness become a true martyrdom of the soul. Once again, we marvel that in 1889, the young Thérèse could write to Céline: "What has Jesus done, then, to detach our souls from all that is created?[33] Ah, He has struck a big blow... but it is a blow of love. God is ad-mirable, but He is especially lovable; let us love Him, then... let us love Him enough to suffer for Him all that He wills, even spiritual pains, aridities, anxieties, apparent coldness.... Ah, here is great love, to love Jesus without feeling the sweetness of this love... this is mar-tyrdom.... Well, then, *let us die as martyrs.*"[34]

Purifications

It is extremely difficult to try to follow the spiritual itinerary of Sr. Thérèse in light of the categories described by St. John of the Cross in *The Ascent of Mount Carmel* and *The Dark Night.* A study in Spanish has tried it. Fr. Marie-Eugène has no problem affirming that "St. Thérèse of the Child Jesus rapidly passed through all the purifications of the senses and the spirit because she never paid at-tention to them."[35]

That Thérèse was purified cannot be doubted. She was well aware of her tendencies, especially towards the self-love that can be said to come from THE original sin: pride.[36] In the meantime she

---

[33] Objective proposed by St. John of the Cross; the allusion is evident.
[34] LT 94 [GC I, p. 577].
[35] *Jean de la Croix, Présence de lumière* [John of the Cross, Presence of light], pp. 231-232.
[36] Cf. M.-D. Molinié, *Je choisis tout* [I choose all], CLD, 1992: "Thérèse et l'orgueil" [Thérèse and pride], pp. 186-192.

ignores the word "purification" in her writings and the verb "to purify" occurs very seldom.[37] "It would certainly happen quickly," Fr.
Marie-Eugène wrote, "in a life that didn't last more than 24 years."

* * *

For ten years — from after the death of her mother (1877) until
her conversion on Christmas 1886 — she lived through a series of
trying purifications, a kind of efficient novitiate that brought her to
detach herself from everything, first of all of from herself. She encountered sufferings interspersed with great graces. Let us resume
this itinerary of a child who suffered a lot.[38]

The death of her mother when Thérèse was four and a half
provoked a wound that would heal only ten years later. The succes-
sive losses of her second Mother (Pauline), then the third (Marie),
reopened this wound. A very serious illness followed Pauline's departure for Carmel and the child would be healed of it only through
the smile of the Virgin Mary (May 13, 1883). But "two wounds to
the soul" remained and she was not relieved of them until four or
five years later. Let us remember that apropos of the pain she felt in
her soul concerning the "Virgin's secret" that she thought she had
betrayed, Thérèse wrote: "the Blessed Virgin permitted this torment
for my soul's good, as perhaps without it I would have had some
thought of vanity, whereas *humiliation* becoming my lot, I was unable to look upon myself without a feeling of *profound horror*. Ah!
what I suffered I shall not be able to say except in heaven!"[39] Thérèse
was now a little more than ten years old. She would have to grow up
in order to get out of this negative feeling. She would have to come
to know reconciliation within herself. This happened in the church

---

[37] Five times in the Manuscripts, three times in the *Letters*, twelve times in the collection of
writings.

[38] "My mind developed in the midst of suffering…" (Ms A, p. 60 [27r°]) and many other
quotations.

[39] Ms A, p. 67 (31r°).

of Our Lady of Victories in Paris, where a Marian grace put her mind fully at rest.[40]

After her second retreat at school for the renewal of her Communion, she entered a crisis of scruples that lasted 17 months. Only her sister Marie could help her to move forward in that fog. Now in October 1886, Marie in turn entered the Carmel in Lisieux. The loss of this third mother caused Thérèse to fall to the darkest bottom. It took the miracle of her "conversion" on Christmas 1886, to truly free her and then allow her to begin "a giant's course" and fight to enter Carmel.

The purifying sufferings did not cease in Carmel. They took on another form because Thérèse had grown and become an adult young woman. The most profound and critical suffering was her beloved father's mental illness, to which we will come back later.

Thérèse did not pick up the vocabulary of St. John of the Cross about purification. But she experienced the reality of active and passive purifications. Was it necessary for her to be purified? Of course, since she was not the Immaculate Conception! She herself recognized her tendency towards self-love[41] which, as Fr. Molinié emphasizes, can degenerate into pride. The rude pedagogy of Mother Marie de Gonzague had spotted this tendency in the novice whom she often humiliated at the beginning of her religious life. Later Thérèse thanked her for it (Ms C, p. 206 [1vº]).

Did Fr. Pichon, who was guiding her, not say in her general confession in May 1888: "…had [God] abandoned you, instead of being a little angel, you would have become a little demon" (Ms A, p. 149 [70rº])?

It is also very important for us to note that "from the beginning, Thérèse's sufferings had a redemptive dimension. Her purification was so painful because the sufferings of her Dark Night were co-redemptive, according to her motive for entering Carmel ('I come,

---

[40] Ms A, p. 66 [30vº], p. 123 [56vº].
[41] Ms A, p. 24 (8rº), p. 158 (73vº), p. 159 (74vº), p. 160 (75rº).

to pray for sinners'). She did not wait to be a saint for her sufferings have this intention, this significance and scope."[42]

Thérèse was very aware of this: *"suffering alone* gives birth to souls" (Ms A, p. 174, [81r°]). She confirmed it on the day of her death: "Never would I have believed it was possible to suffer so much! never! never! I cannot explain this except by the ardent desires I have had to save souls" (CJ 9.30 [HLC, p. 205]).

These purifications began for young Thérèse in 1887 when she experienced — undoubtedly for the first time — three days of distress. Uncle Guérin had refused to allow her to enter Carmel at such a young age.

Listen to his niece: "Before allowing any ray of hope to shine in my soul, God willed to send me a painful martyrdom lasting *three days* [October 19-21]. Oh! never had I understood so well as during this trial, the sorrow of Mary and Joseph during their three-day search for the divine Child Jesus. I was in a sad desert, or rather my soul was like a fragile boat delivered up to the mercy of the waves and having no pilot. I knew that Jesus was there sleeping in my boat, but the night was so black that it was impossible to see Him; nothing gave me any light, not a single flash came to break the dark clouds. No doubt, lightning is a dismal light, but at least if the storm had broken out in earnest I would have been able to see Jesus for one passing moment. But it was night! The dark night of the soul! I felt I was all alone in the garden of Gethsemane like Jesus, and I found no consolation on earth or from heaven; God Himself seemed to have abandoned me!" (Ms A, p. 109 [51r°]).

This text is remarkable on several levels. First, on the level of the vocabulary that Thérèse will always use throughout her life to characterize her prayer: Jesus' sleep, thunderstorm, night, lightning.... But also for the symbol of the "three days," which she underlined and explained: the three days of searching for the Child Jesus in the Temple (cf. PN 54.13 [*Poetry*, p. 217]), the three days of the

---

[42] Molinié, *Je choisis tout* [I choose all], pp. 64-65.

Crucified in the darkness of the Tomb. In both cases, she identifies with Jesus. For her inner story, these three days are decisive: they foretell all the dark nights that will be her everyday experience in Carmel.

It has to be said that these three days appeared so disconcerting to her because she had received significant graces in 1887, that wonderful year following her Christmas conversion. The reading of Arminjon's book,[43] the conversations in the belvédère of Les Buissonets with Céline: "I don't know if I'm mistaken, but it seems to me the outpourings of our souls were similar to those of St. Monica with her son when, at the port of Ostia, they were lost in ecstasy at the sight of the Creator's marvels! It appears we were receiving graces like those granted to the great saints. (…) how *light* and *transparent* the veil was that hid Jesus from our gaze! Doubt was impossible, faith and hope were unnecessary, and *Love* made us find on earth the One whom we were seeking" (Ms A, p. 104 [48r°]).

This is how Faith seems to become unnecessary. Let us repeat that Thérèse appealed to St. John of the Cross in order to describe her progress and Céline's: "in us were realized the words of St. John of the Cross' Canticle (…):

> Following Your footprints,
> Maidens run lightly along the way;
> The touch of a spark,
> The special wine,
> Cause flowings in them from the balsam of God."[44]

Céline, too, remembers these exceptional moments: "Those conversations in the belvédère have left such profound memories that I recall them as if it were yesterday. What Thérèse has written about

---

[43] Cf. the excellent monograph on Blaise Arminjon, *Une soif ardente* [An ardent thirst], DDB-Opéra, 1980, 100 pages; [cf. Ms A, p. 102 (47r°/v°].

[44] Ms A, p. 103 [47v°/48r°], quoting C, stanza 25 [K-RJ, p. 475]. Cf. LT 137 [GC II, pp. 760ff.].

them in the *Story of a Soul*, far from being exaggerated, seems to me to fall short of the actual reality."[45]

It is the period when she "felt within [her] heart certain aspirations unknown until then, and at times [she] had veritable transports of love." She was ready to go "into hell" so that "Jesus would be *loved* eternally in that place of blasphemy. (...) when we experience love, we experience the need of saying a thousand foolish things" (Ms A, p. 112 [52r°]). Later, when she was ill, she recalled: "At the age of fourteen, I also experienced transports of love. Ah! how I loved God!" (CJ 7.7.2 [HLC, p. 77]).

When Fr. Pichon was still at Carmel, he believed her faith to be "entirely childlike" (CJ 7.4.4.).[46] She was plunged into aridity very quickly, as we noticed before.

But we must not neglect some less ordinary graces. Why doesn't she mention them in her first manuscript? We have good reason to believe it is because the manuscript was addressed to Mother Agnès of Jesus. Thérèse knew that her little mother didn't appreciate these realities at all and was very suspicious of them. It is characteristic that a certain number of exceptional graces are found only in *Her Last Conversations*. First, Mother Agnès could not have invented them; secondly, knowing about them, she did not want to pay attention to them. Only when her sister will become seriously, terminally ill, will she insist that Thérèse tell them to her again.

So, Thérèse received these graces during her novitiate:

"She spoke to me about her prayers of former days, in the summer evenings during the periods of silence, and she understood then by experience what a 'flight of the spirit' was.[47] She spoke to me about another grace of this kind which she received in the grotto of St. Mary Magdalene, in the month of July, 1889, a grace followed by several days of 'quietude': [48]

---

[45] MSG, p. 17.

[46] [Cf. HLC, p. 73; Ms A, p. 149 (70r°) — Trans.]

[47] Cf. Teresa of Avila, *The Interior Castle, 6th Mansion*, chap. 5.

[48] Cf. Idem., *The Way of Perfection*, chap. 32.

"'...It was as though a veil had been cast over all the things of earth for me.... I was entirely hidden under the Blessed Virgin's veil. At this time, I was placed in charge of the refectory, and I recall doing things as though not doing them; it was as if someone had lent me a body. I remained that way for one whole week'" (CJ 7.11.2 [HLC, p. 88]).

Thérèse must have written about this to Fr. Pichon, because he responded on October 4, 1889: "I impatiently await the next letter, which will explain to me, I hope, the mysterious grace mentioned in the last one."[49] However, these graces *are* extraordinary.

Soon a great purification happened to Thérèse: the illness of her beloved father, which led to his confinement on February 12, 1889, and lasted for three years. For it wasn't just any kind of illness. The mental disturbance led to great humiliations for the sick man and his family. Rumor had it that the Bon Saveur was an "insane asylum." Gossip was rampant in Lisieux. How could this poor M. Martin not lose his head when all his daughters had became religious! He had been "destroyed" by the departure of the youngest, the most beloved, his "little Queen."

For Thérèse, her father was a "saint," the image of paternal goodness, image of the heavenly Father's goodness. Now he was humiliated, sometimes confused, sometimes lucid, in the midst of hundreds of mentally ill patients. It was now that his youngest daughter discovered another aspect of God. The texts of Lent 1890, revealed to her the passages of Isaiah about the Suffering Servant who is humiliated, going like a sheep to the slaughterhouse.

The greatest trial of her life touched the novice at her most profound depth, at the center of her heart. It was a trial of faith and hope that matured her astonishingly, so much so that she later saw it as a most special grace.

In June of 1888, at the time of her father's first ordeal, she said:

---

[49] DE, p. 466; 7.11.2, note e [French edition]. This shows that Thérèse was writing one letter a month to her Director, telling him about her spiritual life. We know that Fr. Pichon destroyed all the letters of this correspondent.

"'I am suffering very much, but I feel I can still bear greater trials.' I was not thinking then [...] that on February 12 [1889], a month after my reception of the Habit, our dear Father would drink the *most bitter* and *most humiliating* of all chalices. Ah! that day, I didn't say I was able to suffer more! Words cannot express our anguish, and I'm not going to attempt to describe it. One day, in heaven, we shall love talking to one another about our *glorious* trials; don't we already feel happy for having suffered them? Yes, Papa's three years of martyrdom appear to me as the most lovable, the most fruitful of my life; I wouldn't exchange them for all the ecstasies and revelations of the saints. My heart overflows with gratitude when I think of this inestimable *treasure* that must cause a holy jealousy to the angels of the heavenly court" (Ms A, pp. 156-157 [73r°]).

Thus when Thérèse mentioned this "great trial" that became "a great treasure," she found again the figure of St. John of the Cross who had touched her in her youth. Through him she learned about the continual, progressive deepening within herself during these years, in the sense of purifications.

At this point we can reread the testimony of Sr. Marie of the Trinity quoted before (pp. 24ff.). She emphasized that concerning suffering, we twice find the words "purify" and "purification" as necessary realities "in order to arrive at perfect union in love."

Sr. Thérèse was aware of other purifications that marked her journey. Such was the case in January 1890, when her profession was delayed. Not that she had done something wrong, but a postponement was preferred for reasons of her youth and her father's illness. Here is Thérèse's reaction after a moment of disappointment: "One day, during my prayer, I understood that my intense desire to make Profession was mixed with a great self-love." We know that this was a tendency of hers. But the light of self-knowledge was at work within her. "Since I had *given* myself to Jesus to please and console Him, I had no right to oblige Him to do *my will* instead of His own" (Ms A, p. 158 [73v°/74r°]). Thus did the Holy Spirit educate the young Carmelite. Each time she accepted to be purified, she received an increase of grace.

Elsewhere and at different moments of her spiritual journey we can find, by means of her concealed confidences, the traces of various purifications. For example, in October 1891, she very much dreaded the community retreat about to take place, because — she wrote as if in parentheses — "At the time I was having great interior trials of all kinds, even to the point of asking myself whether heaven really existed"[50] (Ms A, p. 173 [80vº]). But another clue, coming from Fr. Pichon, lets us think that at the end of 1892, she was still not free from all scruples.[51] The Jesuit's letter was dated January 20, 1893. Given the long delays in mail between France and Canada, and the overload of correspondence with the priest,[52] Thérèse must have written during the last months of 1892. Fr. Pichon wrote:

"Dear Child of my soul, listen to what I am about to tell you in the name and on the part of Our Lord: No, no, you have not committed any mortal sins. I swear it. No, we cannot sin gravely without knowing it. No, after absolution, we must not doubt our state of grace. To your Mother, St. Teresa, who was praying one day for souls, who were deluding themselves, Our Lord answered: 'My daughter, no one is lost without knowing it perfectly.' Banish, then, your worries. God wills it, and I command it. Take my word for it: Never, never, never have you committed a mortal sin. Go quickly to kneel before the Tabernacle to thank Our Lord. Fall asleep, tranquil and serene in the arms of Jesus. He has never betrayed you; He will never betray you."[53]

---

[50] It is precisely this subject of heaven that will cause her final great ordeal (Ms C, pp. 211-212 [5vº]).

[51] Earlier, in October 1889, he had written: "I forbid you in the name of God to call into question your being in the state of grace. The devil is laughing heartily at you. I protest against this ugly mistrust. Believe obstinately that Jesus loves you" (LC 117 [GC I, p. 585]).

[52] Replying to Sr. Marie of the Sacred Heart, who had written him 14 letters, Fr. Pichon wrote to her that 700 letters were waiting on his desk!

[53] LC 151 [GC II, p. 767].

This document is astonishing, because the Jesuit repeats almost word for word what he had said aloud to Thérèse in May 1888, when she made her general confession (Ms A, p. 149 [70r°]). It is amazing that five years later "she is still there," doubting her state of grace. Her Director had to manifest all his authority to reassure her once again.

Further, the Carmel archives keep a little handwritten note of Thérèse reporting the answer of Fr. Baillon, who was named extraordinary confessor for the monastery at the beginning of 1892. It reads: "If you do not act against your conscience, even though there could be a sin, you would not be sinning." The slanted handwriting and black ink indicate that the note might date from 1893; in any case, surely not before 1892.[54]

Thus we observe that at the age of 20, Thérèse still suffered from scruples that were purifying her. Some commentators situate Sr. Thérèse in the night of the spirit, that of the senses having passed even before her entry into Carmel. We must mention these estimations with prudence, certainly, but they do allow an overview of her journey.

According to the theory of Fr. Conrad De Meester, it was towards the end of 1894 that Thérèse crystallized her discovery of the way of spiritual childhood.[55] The Carmelite priest has shown with utmost precision that the scriptural texts of the Old Testament that provoked this discovery are to be found in one of the notebooks brought by Céline Martin when she entered Carmel on September 14, 1894. (We have already said that one of these notebooks includes a section of texts of St. John of the Cross that was very important for Thérèse.)

The discovery of the little way of spiritual childhood culminated on June 9, 1895, feast of the Holy Trinity, when Thérèse offered herself as a holocaust victim to Merciful Love, "heart of the

---

[54] LC 151 (GC II, p. 768, note 5).

[55] *Dynamique de la confiance*, Cerf, 1995; *The Power of Confidence*, Alba House, 1998.

little way and its logical conclusion."[56] For Fr. Marie-Eugène of the Child Jesus, this act is a "summit." Other commentators, Fr. Molinié for instance, say that this oblation is the equivalent of the transforming union of John of the Cross and the spiritual marriage of the seventh *Mansion* of Teresa of Avila.

Above all, let us not forget the grace that occurred several days later, undoubtedly on Friday, June 14, when Sr. Thérèse was making the Stations of the Cross alone, as was her custom. (We will come back to this at length in Chapter 5.) What is important for us here is to notice the end of her disclosure: "As for me, I experienced it [this fiery dart in the heart] only once and for one single instant, falling back immediately into my habitual state of dryness."[57]

A second response from heaven — very paradoxical — to her Oblation will be this night of Faith and Hope that Thérèse will tell to Mother Marie de Gonzague in her last manuscript of June 9, 1897. It is no accident that the *only* dated text in her manuscripts is this one, written two years to the day after her oblation. On this anniversary she recounted to her prioress that when she had two episodes of spitting up blood in her cell on Holy Thursday and Good Friday 1896, she had no fear whatsoever, but only joy: *"It was like a sweet and distant murmur that announced the Bridegroom's arrival"* (Ms C, p. 211 [4v°]).

She then described the state of her soul before the ordeal: "At this time I was enjoying such a living faith, such a clear *faith*, that the thought of heaven made up all my happiness. I was unable to believe that there were really impious people who had no faith. I believed they were actually speaking against their own inner convictions when they denied the existence of heaven, that beautiful heaven where God Himself wanted to be their Eternal Reward" (Ms C, p. 211 [5r°/5v°]).

Young Thérèse had received the faith from those around her, from family and school: "…the certainty of going away one day far

---

[56] C. De Meester, *Les Mains vides* [Empty Hands], Cerf, 1972, p. 99.

[57] CJ 7.7.2 [HLC, p. 77].

from the sad and dark country had been given me from the day of my childhood. I did not believe this only because I heard from persons much more knowledgeable than I" (this refers to faith received *ex auditu* [from hearing; cf. Rom 10:17]), "but I felt in the bottom of my heart real longings for this most beautiful country" (Ms C, p. 213 [6vº]). This is the seed of faith at the core of her being.

So, "during those very joyful days of the Easter season" [Ms C, p. 211 (5vº)], the brutal entry into the dark night occurred that lasted until September 30, 1897, despite some very brief periods of calm. We need not detail here her account of this ordeal.[58] Let us emphasize the important words: her soul was in "fog," "darkness," in a "tunnel"; there was a "wall" that hid the starry firmament. The voice of sinners mocked her, whispering: "Advance, advance; rejoice in death which will give you not what you hope for but a night still more profound, the night of nothingness" (Ms C, p. 213 [6vº]). The sick nun who would die of tuberculosis was aware that this ordeal was a final purification of the very last traces of her own personality: "Now [this ordeal] is taking away everything that could be a natural satisfaction in my desire for heaven" (Ms C, p. 214 [7vº]).

Yes, final purifications…. We can't challenge Thérèse's own testimony about this. But this ordeal was essentially co-redemptive. Thérèse was acutely aware of this and she voluntarily sat down — with Jesus (Mt 9:10-11) — at the table of sinners. She had, in spirit, overcome all self-interest and could willingly experience even the confusion of "unbelievers." She wanted to stay alone with them so as to pray in their name: *"Have pity on us, O Lord, for we are poor sinners!* [Lk 18:13] Oh! Lord, send us away justified. May all those who were not enlightened by the bright flame of faith one day see it shine. O Jesus! if it is needful that the table soiled by them be purified by a soul who loves You, then I desire to eat this bread of trial

---

[58] Cf. E. Renault, *L'Épreuve de la foi* [The trial of faith], Cerf, 1974 and 1992, and J.-F. Six, *Thérèse de Lisieux et les incroyants* [Thérèse of Lisieux and unbelievers], Institut catholique de Paris, May 1973, pp. 151-165. [See also Frederick L. Miller, *The Trial of Faith of St. Thérèse of Lisieux*, New York: Alba House, 1998.]

at this table until it pleases You to bring me into Your bright King-dom. The only grace I ask of You is that I never offend you!" (Ms C, p. 212 [6r°]).

Thérèse lived her Gethsemane. In the dark night with Christ, who is seated at table with the tax collectors and prostitutes — to the great scandal of the scribes and Pharisees — she accepted this darkness so that the "ungodly" might have light. This is Thérèse's com-passion.[59]

All proportions considered, Thérèse is close to the Virgin Mary standing at the foot of her Son's Cross: this is the com-passion of Mary, model, figure, paradigm of the Church. In May of 1897, Thérèse in her great hymn that became her testament about Mary, mentioned the Virgin's trial of faith:

"Mother, your sweet Child wants you to be the example

> Of the soul searching for Him in the night of faith.
> Since the King of Heaven wanted his Mother
> To be plunged into the night, in anguish of heart,
> Mary, is it thus a blessing to suffer on earth?
> Yes, to suffer while loving is the purest happiness!...
> All that He has given me, Jesus can take back.
> Tell him not to bother with me.....
> He can indeed hide from me, I'm willing to wait for him
> Till the day without sunset when my faith will fade away....."
>
> (PN 54.15,7-8; 16)

Thérèse wrote this poem when she was sick and in the dark night of faith. The poem is about suffering *while loving*. She clearly affirmed — contrary to oft-heard sermons — that the Virgin did know the trial of faith.[60]

John Paul II goes even further in his encyclical *Mother of the Redeemer* (1987): "At the foot of the Cross, Mary participates by faith

---

[59] This voluntary identification with Christ affirms itself during the last months of her ill-ness. Cf. our *Passion of Thérèse of Lisieux* (NY: Crossroad, 1990), pp. 228ff.

[60] DE II, Synopsis, pp. 310-315.

in the shocking mystery of total self-emptying (the Pope goes on to quote Ph 2:5-8). Here, without doubt, is the deepest 'kenosis'[61] of faith in the history of the human race" (n. 36).[62] This is most certainly the boldest phrase in all the studies of Mariology.[63] Of course, Mary of Nazareth's trial of faith was not purifying at all; it was participation in the redemption wrought by her Son.

* * *

Thérèse's trial had reached the peak of suffering. People told her: "What a terrible sickness and how much you're suffering!" - "Yes! What a grace it is to have faith! If I had not had any faith, I would have committed suicide without an instant's hesitation..." (CJ 9.22.6 [HLC, p. 196]).

Fr. Marie-Eugène said: "St. John of the Cross says that even in transforming union, when the soul enjoys peace, it knows suffering, a suffering that is no longer purifying (directed towards herself) but a suffering of radiance (for others), a suffering of the apostolate."[64]

Thérèse waged the battle of faith: "I believe I have made more acts of faith in this past year than all through my whole life" (Ms C, p. 213 [7r°]). She practiced the "anagogical act" described by St. John of the Cross[65] for escaping the devil. "At each new occasion of combat, when my enemies provoke me, I conduct myself bravely. Knowing it is cowardly to enter into a duel, I turn my back on my adversaries without deigning to look them in the face; but I run toward my Jesus. I tell Him I am ready to shed my blood to the last drop to profess my faith in the existence of *heaven*" (Ms C, pp. 213-214 [7r°]). "As soon as you make an act of faith, which St. John calls an

---

[61] [Greek for "self-emptying" — Trans.]

[62] [No. 18 in the English version — Trans.]

[63] In his book *Marie, clé du mystère chrétien* [Mary, key to the Christian mystery], Fayard, 1994, René Laurentin emphasizes several times that the Mariology of Thérèse of Lisieux heralds that of Vatican Council II, pp. 112, 131.

[64] *Retraite* [Retreat], 1935, p. 4.

[65] [Cf. A, 2. 21. 4 (K-RJ, p. 446).]

'anagogical act,' you escape the devil; he no longer understands a thing."[66] Thérèse again speaks about this anagogic act in her canticle *Abandonment Is the Sweet Fruit of Love*:[67]

> No, nothing worries me.
> Nothing can trouble me.
> My soul knows how to fly
> Higher than the lark.

These acts of faith take on different forms. A prayer, for example, written in haste on a piece of paper, says: "My God, with the help of your grace I am ready to shed all my blood to affirm my faith" (Pri 19). A variant reads: "for each of the articles of the Creed."[68]

Fr. Godefroy Madeleine, to whom she confided her ordeal, had recommended to her to write the Creed and carry it on her heart. She wrote it with her blood. She carved on the inside of her cell door: "Jesus, my only Love," a phrase that is common in her poems.[69] She composed "little poems" and people around her thought them filled with consolations. But she "sings simply what she WANTS TO BELIEVE" without feeling "any joy" in it (Ms C, p. 214 [7vº]).

Yes, she is truly a daughter of the one for whom faith is habitually "night," dark and changeless. She obstinately willed to remain in faith, she didn't desire "to see." Vision is reserved for the life beyond this life. On this point she remained unshakable, in spite of her sisters' repeated urgings. Already on October 21, 1895, she had written:

---

[66] Fr. Marie-Eugène of the Child Jesus, *Jean de la Croix, présence de lumière*, p. 181. Cf. N, 2. 21. 4 [K-RJ, p. 446].

[67] PN 52:16 [*Poetry*, p. 208]. An introductory note (*Poetry*, p. 205) indicates about this verse: "Irresistibly, she calls to mind the anagogical act of St. John of the Cross: For the soul assailed by temptation, it is best to soar right up in one leap to God...." ["Anagogical" refers to a spiritual approach or mystical way of responding to a specific situation—Trans.]

[68] Facsimile in *Thérèse et Lisieux*, p. 261 [also in *Prayers*, p. 114 — Trans.].

[69] Cf. PN 15.4,2 [*Poetry*, p. 83]; PN 45.3,6 [p. 186]; PN 36.refrain, 2, 3 [p. 165]. See the inscription in her cell in *Thérèse et Lisieux*, p. 261.

> Remember that on the day of your victory
> You told us, "He who has not seen
> The Son of God all radiant with glory
> Is blessed if still he has believed!"
> In the shadow of Faith, I love you and adore you.
> O Jesus! I'm waiting in peace for the dawn to see you.
>   I don't desire
>   To see you here on earth,
>   Remember.....
>
>   (PN 24.27; cf. sta. 28)

Faith allowed her to contemplate the mystery of the Eucharist:

> Little Key, oh, I envy you!
> For each day you can open
> The prison of the Eucharist
> Where the God of Love resides.
> But, O what a sweet miracle!
> By just an effort of my faith
> I can also open the tabernacle
> To hide near the Divine King...
>
>   (PN 25.1)

She always emphasized and affirmed more fervently this distinction between faith on earth and the actual vision to come beyond death,[70] the closer she approached her end: "I've had a greater desire not to see God and the saints, and to remain in the night of faith, than others have desired to see and understand" (CJ 8.11.5 [HLC, p. 146]). "Oh! no, I don't have any desire to see God here on earth. And yet I love Him! I also love the Blessed Virgin very much, and the saints, and I don't desire to see them" (CJ 9.11.7 [HLC, p. 188]). The edition of *Novissima Verba* adds, "I prefer to live in faith."[71]

---

[70] Cf. the prayer for the feast of Epiphany: "Mercifully grant that we who know you now by faith, may be brought to the clear vision of your glory in heaven."

[71] DE II, p. 177; NV 9.11.5.

In June of 1897 she said to her sisters: "Don't be astonished if I don't appear to you after my death, and if you see nothing extraordinary as a sign of my happiness. You will remember that it's 'my little way' not to desire to see anything. You know well what I've said so often to God, to the angels, and to the saints:

> My desire is not
> To see them here on earth."
> (CJ 6.4.1, quoting PN 24.27)

Later, in August, Sr. Marie of the Sacred Heart told her that when she died the angels would come to her in the company of Our Lord, that she will see them resplendent with light and beauty. The patient responds: "All those images do me no good; I can nourish myself on nothing but the truth. This is why I've never wanted any visions. We can't see, here on earth, heaven, the angels, etc., just as they are. I prefer to wait until after my death" (CJ 8.5.4 [HLC, p. 134]). "Oh! no, I don't have any desire to see God here on earth. And yet I love Him!" (CJ 9.11.7 [HLC, p. 188]). It is revealing that the words "vision" and "ecstasy" are not a normal part of her vocabulary.[72]

Making reference to the "consolations" Céline had received at Lourdes in October 1890, the young Carmelite wrote to Sr. Agnès of Jesus: "I have no desire to go to Lourdes to have ecstasies. I prefer (the monotony of sacrifice)!" (LT 106 [CG I, p. 620]). Besides, was that not the everyday life of the greatest of saints:

> Mother full of grace, I know that in Nazareth
> You live in poverty, wanting nothing more.
> No raptures, miracle, or ecstasy
> Embellish your life, O Queen of the Elect!....
> The number of little ones on earth is truly great.
> They can raise their eyes to you without trembling.

---

[72] In all the manuscripts, the only vision mentioned is the one from her childhood at Les Buissonets, of a man walking along her little garden (Ms A, pp. 45-46 [20r°]).

It's by the *ordinary way*, incomparable Mother,
That you like to walk to guide them to Heaven.
(PN 54.17)

In the recreational drama *The Triumph of Humility*,[73] Thérèse in her sense of humor played her own role as mistress of novices. She put a question to Sr. Marie-Madeleine, who desired "consolations and extraordinary graces." Her prayers were so arid that she "wouldn't mind catching a glimpse of what is going on in heaven. — Don't you know that our Father St. John of the Cross has called it a venial sin to ask for ecstasies and revelations?"[74] Another novice intervenes: "It is a fault... I didn't know that... Oh well! Yet I desire them, too...." The novice mistress then quotes the Gospel: "Happy are those who have not seen and yet believe" (Jn 20:29).[75]

A little later in the same drama, *The Triumph of Humility*, Sr. Thérèse says to the novices who claim to have experienced the devil: "You must go right away to tell Mother Prioress what we've heard..." (scene 5). Yet another time she is obeying the *Maxims* of the Spanish saint: "When God favors some soul with a supernatural revelation, he encourages the soul to share this with one of the ministers of Holy Church, who puts it into context."[76]

This refusal to ask for consolations was affirmed by Thérèse in her letter of September 8, 1896:[77] "Thinking of the mysterious dreams which are granted at times to certain souls, I said of myself that these dreams must be a very sweet consolation, and yet I wasn't asking for such a consolation" (Ms B, p. 190 [2rº]).

---

[73] RP June 7, 1896, 1vº.

[74] Thérèse had read Maxim 34 of John of the Cross: "The soul that wants to have revelations commits at least a venial sin" (p. 15). The saint refers to this thought many times: A, 2. 21 (p. 270 in Thérèse's copy) and 3.30 [K-RJ, pp. 223 and 323]. Cf. A, 2. 19 [K-RJ, p. 218]; MSG, p. 204.

[75] St. John of the Cross recalls this text in A, 2. 11. 12 and 3. 31. 8 [K-RJ, pp. 184 and 327].

[76] No. 187; cf. no. 186, pp. 53-54 in Thérèse's copy.

[77] [This letter has become the first part of Ms B, so is not among the letters in GC II — Trans.]

Céline in her memoirs totally verified her young sister's habitual attitude. After hearing about a comforting dream Céline had about her vocation and her reaction to it, Thérèse replied: "Ah! this is something I never would have done — ask for consolations! Since you want to resemble me, you know as well as I do that I say:

> Oh! Don't fear, Lord, that I'll wake you up.
> I wait peacefully for the Kingdom of Heaven.

"It is so sweet to serve God in the night of trial, we have only this lifetime to live by faith!..."[78]

This constant attitude could be summed up in one astounding declaration that is made in the *Last Conversations*: "(In Heaven) I shall see God, true; but as far as being in His presence, I am totally there here on earth" (CJ 5.15.7 [HLC, p. 45]). The strength of her virtue of faith can't be better expressed. At the doors of death, she is going to see God soon, but she thinks that the vision of him won't bring anything more substantial than what she already has in the earthly plan of things! She identifies faith and vision absolutely, because in both cases union with God is the same. The power and effectiveness of faith can't be described any better! All of this conforms to the little way: "As for me, I have lights only to see my little nothingness. This does me more good than all the lights on the faith " (CJ 8.13 [HLC, p. 148]).

To an extraordinary degree, Thérèse preferred the ordinary. Concerning her manuscripts, when she was told that they will eventually be published, she said, "There will be something in it for all tastes, except for those in extraordinary ways" (CJ 8.9.2 [HLC, p. 143]). In a biography of St. John of the Cross, she had been "struck" by the thought of a contemporary: "Brother John of the Cross! He's a religious who is less than ordinary!" (CJ 8.2.2 [HLC, p. 128]).[79] She couldn't guess that one day Sr. St. Vincent de Paul would say

---

[78] MSG, p. 197.

[79] Cf. "What does me a lot of good when I think of the Holy Family is to imagine a life that was very ordinary" (CJ 8.20.14 [HLC, p. 159]).

the same thing about her: "I don't understand why people talk so much about Sr. Thérèse of the Child Jesus. She did nothing remarkable; we scarcely see her practicing virtue, we can't even say she is a good religious."[80]

Thérèse had wished "to be disregarded," and her wish was granted. She had written, "What a joy to be... *unknown* even to persons with whom you live..." (LT 106). Likewise we will see (Chapter 5) that she wanted only a very ordinary death.

* * *

At the end of this chapter about the theological virtue of faith, we quote Fr. Marie-Eugène of the Child Jesus: "St. Thérèse of the Child Jesus embodies the holiness of our times, a holiness that one may say appears much more by the negative, by impoverishment than by the positive; by an absence of experience rather than by the experience itself. It is pure St. John of the Cross: nothing, nothing, nothing, nothing, nothing. But God's abundance isn't less apparent and isn't less felt than poverty."[81]

"Contemplation isn't extraordinary graces, nor ecstasies, nor experiences of God, but the ability to look itself." Thérèse regarded everything with faith throughout her life. "On the little way of St. Thérèse of Lisieux," wrote Jacques Maritain, "the soul is totally stripped bare, and its prayer itself is stripped bare — so arid sometimes that it seems to flee into distractions and emptiness. It is a way that demands great courage. To abandon yourself to Him whom you love means to take on everything, to go through all the stages that Jesus wants you to go through — it's up to Him to know — and to be led wherever Jesus wants, in light or in darkness."[82]

---

[80] PA, p. 339.

[81] *Retraite* [Retreat], 1961, p. 108.

[82] *Le Paysan de la Garonne* [The Peasant of the Garonne], DDB, 1966, p. 339.

4

THE FOLLY OF HOPE

"My folly is to hope…"

(Ms B, 5rº)

Hope and poverty

IN WHAT CONCERNS THE THIRD THEOLOGICAL VIRtue — the green tunic, according to St. John of the Cross[1] — Sr. Thérèse retained some fundamental principles of her spiritual father. In the arrangement of his writings, Hope is placed as a middle term between Love and Faith. His great lines concerning Love, as we have seen, made a profound impression on her. As for Faith, she lived its essence. As for Hope, closely linked to desire, she found some sayings that she will often return to and which will one day lead her to the discovery of the way of childhood, the way of littleness and confidence.

In the writings of St. John of the Cross she read two very significant counsels:

> *"The more God wants to give us, the more He increases our desires, even making the soul empty so that He can refill it with His goods (no. 45). God is so pleased with the hope of a soul that is unceasingly turned towards Him without ever lowering her eyes*

---

[1]   N, 2. 21. 3 (K-RJ, p. 446).

to another object, that in truth it can be said of her: She obtains as
much as she hopes for" (no. 46).[2]

At this point we must add one of the Spanish saint's sentences
in a letter to Mother Eleanor of St. Gabriel: "The more he wants to
give, the more he makes us desire (even to the point of leaving us
empty in order to fill us with goods)."[3] The first part of this phrase
is to be found in the *Act of Offering to Merciful Love*: "I am certain,
then, that you will grant my desires; I know, O my God! That *the*
more you want to give, the more you make us desire." The italics indicate the quotation (Pri 6).

This certitude became one of the pillars in her line of thought
concerning the discovery of the little way. For her it was a basic prin-
ciple: "God cannot inspire unrealizable desires. I can, then, in spite
of my littleness, aspire to holiness" (Ms C, p. 207 [2v°]). In the same
manuscript we can read: "Ah, the Lord is so good to me that it is
quite impossible for me to fear Him. He has always given me what
I desire or rather He has made me desire what He wants to give me"
(Ms C, p. 250 [31r°]).

Thérèse was speaking from experience; throughout her short
life, she experienced the unexpected fulfillment of her desires. At
the age of ten she was healed by the Smiling Virgin. On Christmas
Day 1886, she was freed from her hypersensitivity. The assassin
Pranzini's sudden reversal[4] answered her insistent prayer. She wanted
to enter Carmel at the age of 15; the Lord made her wait only an
additional three months. Wanting snow on her clothing day could
look like a childish fancy, yet she got her wish (Ms A, p. 154/55
[72r°]). In Carmel one of her most astonishing and seemingly impossible desires was for her sister Céline to enter this convent where
her three sisters already lived. Sr. Aimée, the most adamant oppo-

---

[2] Cf. Céline's notebook, VT 78, p. 151.

[3] Letter XI, of 7/8/1589 [K-RJ, p. 750]; Thérèse's copy, vol. I, p. 33. Cf. A, 2.7.11 [K-RJ,
   p. 172] and N 2. 21 (K-RJ, pp. 446-449).

[4] [When he turned to the crucifix just before dying, having rejected belief in God until
   that moment of conversion — Trans.]

nent, would eventually change her mind (Ms A, p. 178 [82vº]) and on September 14, 1894, Céline Martin in turn entered the cloister![5] Thérèse can rightly cry out: "Ah! How many things I have to thank Jesus for; He answers all my requests!" (Ms A, p. 178 [82vº]).[6]

Even wishes that seemed beyond the impossible were fulfilled in unexpected ways. Thérèse had lost *two* young brothers at an early age. She dreamed for them — as did her parents — to be priests and missionaries. Behold, in 1895 (when Mother Agnès was prioress) and 1896 (when Mother Marie de Gonzague was prioress), Thérèse was entrusted with *two* missionaries, the Fathers Bellière and Roulland. She experienced a very deep joy about this, similar to the "great joys" of her childhood (Ms C, p. 251 [31vº/32rº]).

Thus her whole life had been a rhythm composed of her desires and their fulfillment, bringing out the tenderness of Merciful Love shown to her. She could write to Fr. Roulland: "More than ever, I understand that the smallest events of our life are conducted by God; He is the One who makes us desire and who grants our desires...."[7] On June 9, 1897 Thérèse confessed: "I no longer have any great desires except that of loving to the point of dying of love" (Ms C, p. 214 [7vº]). (We will come back to this in Chapter 5.)

In the infirmary she began to hope for a posthumous universal mission. She estimated that she hadn't accomplished anything great before her death. Would she abandon the Church militant? This is when a wild thought arose in her, to "do good after her death." Was this a dream? Delirium from the patient's high fever? There again the doctrine of St. John of the Cross will help her. She prayed, making a novena to St. Francis Xavier known as a "novena of grace" (March 4-12, 1897), considered always efficacious. She added to it a prayer to St. Joseph.

---

[5]   [Wanting Céline to enter was only half of her desire: this entrance was to serve as a sign of reassurance that their father had gone straight to heaven — Trans.]

[6]   Cf. "He didn't want me to have one single desire unfulfilled" (Ms A, pp. 174-175 [81rº]).

[7]   LT 201 [GC II, p. 1015].

On July 13, she wrote to Fr. Bellière and promised to help him from heaven, *until the last day of his life*: "All these promises, Brother, may perhaps appear to you a little bit chimerical; however, you must begin to realize that God has always treated me like a spoiled child. It is true that His Cross has followed me from the cradle, but this Cross Jesus has made me love with a passion. He has always made me desire what He wanted to give me. Will He begin, then, in heaven to carry out my desires no longer? Truly, I can't believe it, and I say: 'Soon, little Brother, I shall be near you.'"[8]

This same day in the infirmary, Thérèse said these very same words to Mother Agnès of Jesus: "God made me always desire what He wanted to give me" (CJ 7.13.15 [HLC, p. 94]). Several days later, she continued to reflect on this subject: "God would not have given me the desire of doing good on earth after my death, if He didn't will to realize it; He would rather have given me the desire to rest in Him" (CJ 7.18.1 [HLC, p. 102]).

She would die with this hope, despite the devil's short-lived temptations and attacks: "I want to do good after my death, but I will not be able to do so! It will be as it was for Mother Geneviève: we expected to see her work miracles and complete silence fell over her tomb...."[9]

With the passing of time, we know that Thérèse has been heard beyond all her hopes: she is spending her heaven of almost one hundred years "doing good on earth until the end of the world" (CJ 7.17 [HLC, p. 102]).

But when she was still on earth, she felt only her poverty. Poverty and hope are intimately connected; whoever has everything no longer hopes for anything. Sr. Thérèse experienced her powerlessness to become a saint, which was nevertheless her hope, based on the requirements of the Gospel. She saw herself poor, little, "a grain of sand" next to the saints who are giants. She knew that "it is im-

---

[8]   LT 253 [GC II, p. 1140].

[9]   HLC pp. 257-258.

possible for me to grow up" (Ms C, p. 207 [2vº]). How many times did she try! Must she renounce holiness, then? This would actually be giving in to discouragement or resignation. But, she wrote keenly, "discouragement is also pride. Therefore, O my God, I want to base my hope in *You alone*."[10]

God alone: nothing else. Hope would be purified and wouldn't be able to lean on anything human. From this came the total renunciation, emptiness and poverty that would aspire to Merciful Love. Thérèse operated on total renunciation; it's a matter not of "gaining but losing," not of rising but "descending."[11] Not only must we "remain little" in order to be taken into "the arms of Jesus," but we must also "become even smaller and smaller." Here is the mark of genius. John the Baptist said, "He must increase and I must decrease" (Jn 3:30).

Let us again read Maxim 45 of John of the Cross, so dear to the Carmelite nun: "The more God wants to give to us, the more He increases our desires, even making the soul empty so that He can refill it with His goods."

The way of spiritual childhood implies the need for poverty (St. John of the Cross's radical privation) and hope in the intervention of God, whose infinite mercifulness doesn't tolerate the emptiness thus achieved in the soul. "The poorer you are the more Jesus will love you," Thérèse wrote to Céline. "He will go far, very far, in search of you, if at times you wander off a little" (LT 211 [GC II, p. 1038]).

"[What] pleases God in my little soul (…) *is that He sees me loving my littleness* and my *poverty, the blind hope* that *I have* in *His mercy….* That is my only treasure," explained Thérèse to her sister Marie of the Sacred Heart in the famous letter of September 17, 1896

---

[10] Pri 20 [*Poetry*, p. 116].

[11] LT 137 [GC II, p. 760ff.]. Cf. LT 165 [GC II, p. 860ff.]. Cf. the writings of A. Louf on the Christian spiritual life, which is not unlimited ascent, but descent, the ladder of true progress being the one of humility according to Rule of St. Benedict: *Au gré de sa grâce* [At the mercy of his grace], DDB, 1989, pp. 75-77.

(LT 197 [GC II, p. 999]). She continued: "to love Jesus, to be His *victim of love*; the weaker one is, without desires or virtues, the more suited one is for the workings of this consuming and transforming Love...."[12] The *desire* alone to be a victim suffices, but we must consent to remain always poor and without strength, and this is the difficulty, for: 'The truly poor in spirit, where do we find him? You must look for him from afar,' said the psalmist.[13]... He does not say that you must look for him among great souls, but 'from afar,' that is to say in *lowliness*, in *nothingness*.... Ah! let us remain then *very far* from all that sparkles, let us love our littleness, let us love to feel nothing, then we shall be poor in spirit, and Jesus will come to look for us, and *however far* we may be, He will transform us in flames of love.... (...) It is confidence and nothing but confidence that must lead us to Love...."

One month before her death, she wrote to Fr. Bellière in the same vein: "Ah, how little known are the *goodness*, the *merciful love* of Jesus, Brother!... It is true, to enjoy these treasures one must humble oneself, recognize one's nothingness, and that is what many souls do not want to do; but, little Brother, this is not the way you act, so the way of simple and loving confidence is really made for you" (LT 261 [GC II, p. 1165]).

She wrote the same message to Céline who, on June 7, 1897, was getting impatient while taking three final photographs of the sick Thérèse:

"We surprise ourselves at times by desiring what sparkles. So let us line up humbly among the imperfect, let us esteem ourselves as *little souls* whom God must sustain at each moment. When He sees we are very much convinced of our nothingness, He extends His hand to us. If we still wish to attempt doing something *great* even under the pretext of zeal, Good Jesus leaves us all alone. 'But when

---

[12] "The Fire of Love is more sanctifying than the one of purgatory" (Ms A, p. 181 [84vº]).

[13] It was in fact from the *Imitation of Christ*, II,11:4 (Thomas à Kempis, the *Imitation of Christ*, adapted by Sister Halson J. Fisk, Catholic Book Publishing New York, 1994, Book 2, Ch. 11, 4, p. 48).

I said "My foot has stumbled," your mercy, Lord, strengthened me!...' (Ps 93:18). Yes, it is enough to humble oneself, to bear with one's imperfections. That is real sanctity!" (LT 243 [CG II, p. 1122]).

In 1925 Sr. Marie of the Trinity, writing to Mother Agnès, commented on this letter in these words: "What canonized saint has ever spoken this way: 'We ourselves,' she said to me, 'we are not saints who cry over our sins; we take delight in them because they serve to glorify the mercy of God.'"[14]

Sr. Thérèse didn't write any treatise about spiritual childhood. After she died, many had to work out syntheses, from whence come some differences in the presentation of this way. We have already quoted Cardinal Daniélou's strong definition: "Spiritual childhood is the infinity of desire within total powerlessness."[15]

The notions of "audacious confidence," of "reckless audacity," "blind offering of self," "without any limits," humility, blend in with poverty to lead to this specific attitude of Thérèse, this way that owes so much to the theological virtue of Hope so dear to John of the Cross.

What is not without humor, if we dare say so, is that Thérèse did not explicitly recognize this influence. To Sr. Marie of the Trinity she confided: "It is God alone who instructed me. No book, no theologian has taught me and nevertheless I feel at the bottom of my heart that I am in the truth. I have not received encouragement from anybody, and when the occasion did come to open my soul, I received so little understanding that I said to God, like St. John of the Cross: 'Do not send me any more messengers, they cannot tell me what I must hear.'"[16]

Charles Péguy, eulogist of hope, who was born five days after Thérèse, didn't read his contemporary, but he wrote in *"The Mystery of the Holy Innocents"*:

---

[14] LT 243 [GC II, p. 1122, note 5].

[15] In the infirmary of the Carmel in Lisieux, August 21,1969: AL no. 10, October 1969, p. 13.

[16] P. Descouvemont, *Thérèse of Lisieux and Marie of the Trinity*, p. 76; quoting C, 6. 3-5 (K-RJ, p. 498). Cf. PA, p. 480 and VT 74, pp. 153-154 with slight variations.

That man pleases me, says God
The one who rests on my arm like a suckling infant who laughs,
And is not concerned with anything.
And who sees the world in his mother's eyes...
... that one pleases me, says God.
The one who abandons himself, I love.
The one who does not abandon himself, I don't love,
It's that simple.
(...)
I know man very well, it is I who made him.
He has a lot of faith and a lot of charity
But what you can't ask of him
Is a little bit of hope
A little confidence, you know, a little relaxation,
a little yielding, a little abandonment
into my hands.
A little giving in.[17]

This childhood has the same tonality as Thérèse's. After several years of Carmelite life, she wrote in 1895: "I always feel, however, the same bold confidence of becoming a great saint because I don't count on my merits since I have *none*, but I trust in Him who is Virtue and Holiness. God alone, content with my weak efforts, will raise me to Himself and make me a *saint*, clothing me in His infinite merits" (Ms A, p. 72 [32r°]).

The young Carmelite always contrasted "great" and "little" souls: "it is sufficient to recognize one's nothingness and to abandon oneself as a child into God's arms. Leaving to great souls, to great minds the beautiful books I cannot understand, much less put into practice, I rejoice at being little since children alone and those who resemble them will be admitted to the heavenly banquet. I am very happy there are many mansions in God's kingdom, for if there were only the one whose description and road seem incomprehensible to me, I would not be able to enter there" (LT 226 [GC II, p. 1094]).

---

[17] "Abandonment," *God Speaks* (New York: Pantheon Books Inc., 1943), pp. 32-35.

To Sr. Marie of the Trinity, disconsolate that she could no longer visit her sick novice mistress, Thérèse gave this advice: "God is calling you to be a great saint while you remain *little* and become more so each day" (LT 242 [GC II, p. 1120]). The Lord uses this littleness, this radical feebleness, to show his power: "He will use this weakness even to carry out His work, for the strong God loves to show His power by making use of nothing" (LT 220 [GC II, p. 1059]).[18] We find again a key saying of St. John of the Cross: "He... uses the weakest instruments to work marvels!" (LT 201 [GC II, p. 1015]).

Another way for Thérèse to speak about her littleness is to evoke her "little nothingness." For example: "It is to God alone that all value must be attributed; there is nothing of value in my little nothingness" (CJ 8.8.1).[19] Granted, this word doesn't have a philosophical meaning here, but it indicates the "non-being" of the creature before its Creator, who alone IS.

* * *

Thus what characterizes Sr. Thérèse of the Child Jesus is her virtue of ardent Hope and unfailing Faith, joined together in a burning Love that is usually not *felt*. "You love St. Augustine, St. Magdalene, these souls to whom 'many sins were forgiven because they loved much.' I love them too, I love their repentance, and especially... their loving audacity!"[20]

In the parable of the little bird before her brother eagles, she emphasized her extravagant audacity: "my own *folly* is this: to trust that Your Love will accept me as a victim... My *folly* consists in begging the eagles, my brothers" (the great saints) "to obtain for me the favor of flying towards the Sun of Love with the *Divine Eagle's* (Jesus') *own wings*" (Ms B, p. 200 [5v°]). "Perhaps this is boldness?"

---

[18] Cf. this is what St. Paul said about God's power in man's weakness, 2 Cor 12:1-10.

[19] [HLC, p. 141]; cf. Ms C, p. 206 [2r°]; CJ 8.6.8 [HLC, p. 138].

[20] LT 247 to Fr. Bellière [GC II, p. 1133].

Thérèse asked herself. "No, for a long time you permitted me to be bold with you. You have said to me as the father of the prodigal son said to his older son: '*EVERYTHING that is mine is yours*'" (Ms C, pp. 255-256 [34v°]).

The hidden life with the hidden God

This reality of Sr. Thérèse's hidden life, resembling the hidden life of Christ, could be linked to the virtue of Hope, but it is clearly connected to Faith. For we go forward in Faith and one day what is hidden will be revealed (cf. Col 3:3). We are "on the way," en route towards face-to-Face vision. Then Faith and Hope will vanish; nothing but Love will remain.

We can imagine the joy Sr. Thérèse experienced in reading the first verse of the *Spiritual Canticle* —

> Where have you hidden,
> Beloved, and left me moaning?

— and especially its commentary. This contains the quotation from Isaiah 45:15, "Indeed, you are a hidden God," that she quoted so often.[21]

God hides Himself in the innermost recesses of the soul; this is His dwelling within the heart of the baptized person. Thérèse was familiar with this reality: "I have frequently noticed that Jesus doesn't want me to lay up *provisions*; He nourishes me at each moment with a totally new food; I find it within me without my knowing how it is there. I believe it is Jesus Himself hidden in the depth of my poor little heart: He is giving me the grace of acting within me, making me think of all He desires me to do at the present moment" (Ms A, p. 165 [76r°]).

---

[21] [K-RJ, p. 479]; cf. RP 2, 4v°/5r°; RP 6, 1r°; PN 19.1 [*Poetry*, p. 106]; PN 40.9 [p. 171]; Pri 7 [*Prayers*, p. 75].

For Sr. Thérèse, the hidden life of Jesus isn't limited to His life in Nazareth before the time of His preaching. For her, it is the entirety of Jesus' life, from birth to death, that is hidden. She wrote: "the nature of love is to humble itself" (Ms A, p. 14 [2v°]; cf. Ms B, p. 194 [3v°]), evoking the "kenosis" of Ph 2:7. She had read in the *Spiritual Canticle*: "If (God...) had not gazed at us and loved us first (...) and descended, the hair of our lowly love would not have taken him prisoner" (commentary on sta. 31, [K-RJ, p. 598]). She sees three degrees in this self-lowering:

Evidently, Jesus is hidden in the mystery of His Incarnation:

> O God, hidden beneath the features of a Child!
> I behold you radiant
> And already triumphant!   (RP 2, 4v)

Faith and Hope recognize the Word of God in the Baby in the manger.

Likewise, the Crucified on Calvary is hidden from men's eyes: "He humbled Himself in such a way that His face was hidden."[22]

The third degree of abasement is the Eucharist where Jesus is hidden under the completely inadequate appearances of bread and wine. Thérèse was very sensitive to this, especially in her poetry:

> The hidden God of the tabernacle
> Who also hides in our hearts (PN 40.9,1 [*Poetry*, p. 171])

> You live for me, hidden in a host (PN 17.3,3 [*Poetry*, p. 90])[23]

> Divine Jesus, here is the ultimate limit of your love...
>   (RP 2, 5v°)

---

[22] LT 137 [GC II, p. 762], alluding to Isaiah 53:3.

[23] Cf. "Hidden beneath the appearances of a white host" (Ms B, p.199 [5v°]) and "Now in the Sacred Host I see you at the height of you annihilations" (Pri 20 [*Prayers*, p. 115]). Cf. what Pascal wrote to Mlle de Roannez (October 1656) about this "hidden manna." Cf. J. Briend, *Le Dieu caché, Dieu dans l'Écriture* [The hidden God, God in Scripture], Cerf, 1990, p. 92.

Sr. Thérèse is thus a living tabernacle. The request in her *Act of Offering* is understandable: "Remain in me as in a tabernacle and never separate yourself from your little host" (Pri 6 [*Prayers*, p. 54]).

In continuing to read the *Spiritual Canticle* by St. John of the Cross, Thérèse encountered this passage:

> *If you want to find a hidden treasure you must enter the hiding place secretly, and once you have discovered it, you will also be hidden as the treasure is hidden. Since, then, your beloved Bridegroom is the treasure hidden in a field for which the wise merchant sold all his possessions* (Mt 13:44), *and that field is your soul, in order to find him you should forget all your possessions and all creatures and hide in the secret inner room of your spirit....*[24]

Writing to Céline, Thérèse echoed the following passage of St. John of the Cross: "Jesus is a *hidden* treasure, an inestimable good which few souls can find, for it is *hidden*, and the world loves what sparkles. (...) To find a hidden thing one must hide oneself; our life must then be a *mystery*. We must be like Jesus, Jesus whose *face was hidden*" (LT 145 [GC II, p. 809]).

This orientation determines the thérésian spirituality of her cloistered life, her face hidden beneath the black veil: "Make me Resemble you, Jesus..." (Pri 11 [*Prayers*, p. 89]), because she needed more than imitation. The hidden life of Jesus the Beloved instigated the hidden life of the Carmelite:

> You live for me, hidden in a host
> I want to hide myself for you, O Jesus!
> (PN 17.3 [*Poetry*, p. 90])

because "Carmel was the *desert* where God wanted me to go also to hide myself" (Ms A, p. 58 [26rº]).

Quite often she came back to this fundamental reality of her

---

[24] Commentary on stanza 1.9, p. 115 in Thérèse's copy of the works of John; cf. K-RJ, p. 480.

life, under different aspects: "Until my coming to Carmel, I had never fathomed the depth of the treasures hidden in the Holy Face (...) the mysteries of love hidden in the Face of our Spouse... (...) true wisdom consists in 'desiring to be unknown and counted as nothing' (*Imitation* Chap.1, 2:3). (...) Ah! I desired that, like the face of Jesus, 'my face be truly hidden, that no one on earth would know me' (Is 53:3). I thirsted after suffering and I longed to be forgotten." (Ms A, p. 152 [71r°]).

Since her entry into Carmel, she wanted only to be "a little grain of sand, truly unknown, truly hidden from all eyes, that Jesus alone may be able to see it, and that it may become smaller and smaller" (this is already the formula of the little way!), "that it may be reduced to *nothing*...."[25]

"What a jot to be so hidden that nobody thinks of you!... To be *unknown* even to persons with whom you live...."[26]

"He, the King of kings, humbled Himself in such a way that His face was hidden, and no one recognized Him... and I, too, want to hide my face, I want my Beloved alone to see it...."[27]

To her sister Céline who made her profession on February 24, 1896, she offered a diploma parchment illustrated with the *Coat of Arms of Céline*, whom she called "KNIGHT OF LOVE OF SUFFERING AND CONTEMPT." (We again find: "to suffer and to be despised.") Jesus speaks to Céline: "Here below, My Face is hidden, but she can recognize me.... In return, I am placing on her head today the helmet of salvation and grace so that her face may be hidden like Mine.... I will that she hides the gifts she has received from Me, allowing me to give them to her or take them back, just as I please, not attaching herself to a single one, forgetting even all that can make her great in her own eyes and in those of creatures."[28]

---

[25] LT 49 (GC I, p. 427).

[26] LT 106 (GC I, p. 620).

[27] LT 137 (GC II, p. 762). We find 18 citations of Isaiah 53:3 (the hidden face) in the writings of Sr. Thérèse of the Holy Face!

[28] LT 183 (GC II, p. 933).

The places where Thérèse hides herself reveal themselves un-expectedly:
— sometimes in the face of Jesus, echoing St. John of the Cross: "You remain hidden while you dwell in the soul. And by this means, you hide them in the secret refuge of your Face (which is the Word) in order to secure them from the worries of men"[29]
— sometimes in his arms: "It's into your arms that I run and hide"[30]
— or in his heart: "Ah! let me hide in your Heart!..."[31]
— or again in the tabernacle[32]
— and under the mantle of the Holy Virgin.[33]

The works themselves that have been accomplished by the dis-ciple must remain hidden. John of the Cross and Thérèse quote the same verse from the Gospel of St. Matthew: "But when you give alms, your left hand must not know what your right hand is doing... so that your almsgiving may be secret; your Father who sees in se-cret will reward you" (Mt 6:3-4).

The Spanish Carmelite comments: "To avoid this kind of harm, then, these persons must hide their work so that only God might see it, and they should not want anyone to pay attention to it. Not only should they hide it from others, but even from themselves: They should desire neither the complacency of esteeming their work as if it had value, nor the procurement of satisfaction. This is the meaning of our Savior's words: *'Let not the left hand....'*"[34]

Sr. Thérèse comments: "It is true that in reading certain tales of chivalry, I didn't always understand the *realities* of *life*; but God made me feel that true glory is that which will last eternally, and to reach it, it isn't necessary to perform striking works but to hide one-

---

[29] F, commentary on sta. 3.3 (K-RJ, p. 674). Cf. PN 11.3,4 [*Poetry*, p. 73]; PN 12.8,1 [p. 75]; PN 16.1,1 [p. 85]; PN 20.5,3 [p. 110]; Pri 12 [*Prayers*, p. 91].

[30] PN 36.3.2 [*Poetry*, p. 165].

[31] PN 33.3.4 [*Poetry*, p. 156]; cf. PN 23.7.7 [p. 120].

[32] PN 25.1 [*Poetry*, p. 133].

[33] Ms A, p. 123 (57r°); LT 103; PN 1.1.5 [*Poetry*, p. 37]; PN 12.9.4 [p. 75]).

[34] A, 3. 28. 6 (K-RJ, pp. 319-320).

self and practice virtue in such a way that the left hand knows not what the right is doing" (Ms A, p. 72 [31vº/32rº]).

"O my God! But if my suffering was really unknown to You, which is impossible, I would still be happy to have it, if through it I could prevent or make reparation for one single sin against *faith*" (Ms C, p. 214 [7rº]). Here is apostolic concern before all else.

In the *Last Conversations*, it is the same concern to hide her deeds: "It is impossible, I know, but if God were not to see my good actions, I would not be the least bit disturbed by it. I love Him so much that I'd like to please Him without His being aware of it. When He knows it and sees it, He is obliged to reward me, and I don't want Him to have to go to this trouble" (CJ 5.9.3, [HLC, p. 43]).

The hidden life excludes any idea of doing dazzling things. We can't be amazed when Thérèse puts these words into the mouth of St. Joseph: "Then this God of goodness and mercifulness will lavishly reward not only the dazzling actions accomplished for Him, but also the simple desires to serve and to love Him, because He sees everything; his eye penetrates to the bottom of our hearts, the most secret thoughts are not hidden from Him."[35]

These lines well express the spirituality of Thérèse at this time, especially at the end of 1895 and the beginning of 1896. About the little bird (herself) she wrote: "Astounding works are forbidden to her" (Ms B, p. 196 [4rº]).

To poor Sr. Marie of St. Joseph, the nun in charge of the linen room who had such a difficult character that nobody wanted to work with her, Thérèse writes (she had volunteered to help with her work): "The most *painful*, the most LOVING martyrdom is ours since Jesus alone sees it. It will never be revealed to creatures on earth, but when the Lamb will open the *book of life*,[36] what a surprise for the Heavenly Court to hear proclaimed with the names of missionaries and martyrs those of poor little children who will have never performed dazzling actions...."[37]

---

[35] RP 6, 9rº.

[36] Cf. Rv 20:12.

[37] LT 195 (GC II, p. 991).

This whole attitude truly accords with the meaning of the re-
mark by Saint John: "The soul replies to all those who impugn her
holy idleness and desire every work to be the kind that shines out-
wardly and satisfies the eye...."[38]

Finally, it is God's action in the human being that is hidden;
it happens *unknown to herself.* Thérèse goes on... she doesn't know
how: it is the Holy Spirit's secret. "Without showing Himself, without making His voice heard, Jesus teaches me in secret" (Ms B, p.
187 [1r°]). "(Jesus) communicates Himself to souls only as
veiled...."[39] "I understand and I know from experience that: *The king-*
dom of God is within you' (Lk 17:21). Jesus has no need of books or
teachers to instruct souls; He teaches without the noise of words.
Never have I heard Him speak, but I feel that He is within me at
each moment; He is guiding and inspiring me with what I must say
and do" (Ms A, p. 179 [83v°]).

God reveals himself to little ones and not to the wise and
learned. Thérèse quotes this passage from the Gospel of St. Luke
(10:21) when she remembers her youth. "Ah! had the learned who
spent their life in study come to me, undoubtedly they would have
been astonished to see a child of fourteen understand perfection's
secrets, secrets all their knowledge cannot reveal because to possess
them one has to be poor in spirit!" She also adds: "As St. John of
the Cross writes in his Canticle:

> With no other light or guide
> Than the one that burned in my heart;
> This guided me
> More surely than the light of noon
> To where He waited for me."[40]

---

[38] C, introduction to sta. 29, p. 402 in Thérèse's edition [K-RJ, p. 588].

[39] LT 140 [GC II, p. 781]; cf. PN 33.3 [*Poetry*, p. 156]; NEC, p. 416.

[40] Ms A, p. 105 [49r°] quoting N, stanzas 3 and 4 [K-RJ, p. 51]. Cf. Cf. *Carnet scripturaire*
de Thérèse [Biblical notes of Thérèse] in VT 78, April 1980, p. 152. Thérèse replaced the
word "goal/end" with "place," meaning Carmel. An example of adapting the text of St.
John of the Cross to her own situation.

The word *to hide*, in relation to God and Thérèse, appears 212 times in the writings of the Carmelite nun! This is mentioned in order to emphasize the wealth of quotations concerning the Redemptive Incarnation, the Eucharist and Thérèse's attitude.

But everything that is hidden must one day be "revealed,"[41] according to St. Paul's promise: "For you have died and from now on your life is hidden with Christ in God. When Christ will be revealed, who is your life, then you also will be revealed in all your glory with him" (Col 3:3-4).

* * *

At the heart of the little way is Hope. Perhaps this is the most characteristic theological virtue of the young Carmelite: "What offends (Jesus), and what wounds His Heart is the lack of confidence!..." (LT 92 [GC I, p. 568]). "O Jesus, allow me in my boundless gratitude to say to You that Your *love reaches unto folly*. In the presence of this folly, how can You not desire that my heart leap towards You? How can my confidence, then, have any limits?" (Ms B, p. 200 [5vº]).

To the folly of Jesus who loves man unto death, even death on the cross (Ph 2:8), responds the folly of Thérèse who crosses the threshold of Hope to rejoin her Beloved beyond illness, beyond the night of Faith, beyond death: "my *folly* is to hope..." (idem.).[42]

---

[41] A word that Thérèse uses in *Last Conversations*, CJ 7.10.4 [HLC, p. 85].

[42] Cf. our article "Folles aux yeux du monde" ["Fools in the eyes of the world"], *Carmel*, 1976/4, pp. 313-320, about the "folly" of Thérèse, echo of the "folly" of Jesus and St. Paul. Cf. especially LT 169 and PN 17.13 "Living on Love, what a strange folly!..." [The French word *espérer* means "to hope," although the ICS translation reads: "my own *folly* is this: to trust..." (p. 200) — Trans.]

5

TO DIE OF LOVE IN THE LIVING FLAME

"This is my prayer,
I ask Jesus to draw me
into the flames of His love."

Thérèse (Ms C, p. 257 [36rº])

THÉRÈSE HAD NOW ARRIVED AT THE END OF HER life. It is the period of her *Last Conversations* with Mother Agnès of Jesus and her sisters, from April to September 30, 1897. Little by little she abandoned all the common exercises of community life. She stayed either in her cell or in the garden during the beautiful summer afternoons. After July 8, she was brought down to the infirmary (dedicated to the Holy Face) and wouldn't be leaving it again.

Her physical condition became more and more grave.[1] She could no longer read, she prayed with difficulty. However, we have said that it is extremely important for our purpose to know that at her bedside she had the *Spiritual Canticle* and *The Living Flame of Love* in a single volume, and the *Maxims and Spiritual Advice* by John of the Cross.[2]

Two great realities of St. John of the Cross mark this last stage of her life: the consuming fire of love and the death of love.

---

[1] Cf. Guy Gaucher, *The Passion of Thérèse of Lisieux* (New York: Crossroad, 1998), pp. 82ff.

[2] For the references, cf. DE, pp. 843-844 [HLC, p. 246, footnote]. And see the Bibliography at the end of this book.

"Consuming and transforming Love"

This reality was present in her Carmelite life from 1894 on, especially in 1895, but it gained a prominent place under the influence of her even partial reading of *The Living Flame of Love*. At the end of Sr. Thérèse's life, St. John of the Cross, "the Saint of Love par excellence," took pride of place.

Let us go back again to the key phrase that we find specifically in her *Last Conversations* in July, after having written it several times: "With what longing and what consolation I repeated from the beginning of my religious life these other words of our father St. John of the Cross: 'It is of the highest importance that the soul practice Love very much in order that, being consumed rapidly, she may be scarcely retained here on earth but promptly reach the vision of her God face to Face'" (CJ 7.27.5 [HLC, p. 113]).

The fire is first and foremost the furnace of Trinitarian Love (Ms B, p. 200 [5v°]). The creature, like the "dewdrop," longs to be absorbed "in the bosom of the burning furnace of uncreated love" (LT 141 [GC II, p. 785]).[3] This Divine Fire is also Jesus who, like the burning bush, "burns without consuming" (Ms A, p. 83 [38v°] and F, sta. 2 [K-RJ, p. 52]). Jesus has come to enkindle this fire of love on the earth, and His greatest desire is that it consume everything (cf. Lk 12:49).[4]

Thérèse also compares God to the sun. The most characteristic passage dates from the summer of 1896. Identifying herself with the little bird that can't fly, she dares to fix her gaze on the Divine Sun, the Sun of Love. At the center of this Sun she lovingly beholds the Divine Eagle (Christ), the One who takes her upon his wings

---

[3] On God who is fire cf. M. Cocagnac, *Les Symboles bibliques, lexique théologique* [Biblical symbols *in* Theological lexicon], 1993, pp. 30-35 and B. Renaud, "YHWH, ton Dieu est un feu dévorant" ["Yahweh your God is a devouring fire"], *Vie spirituelle*, num. 712, 1994, pp. 583-600.

[4] Thérèse quotes this verse seven times; cf. BT, pp. 217-218.

and brings her into the Eternal Furnace of the Blessed Trinity (Ms B, pp. 198-200 [5vº]).[5]

We touch here upon the highest vocation of man created in the image of God. "One day I hope that You, the Adorable Eagle, will come to fetch me, Your little bird; and ascending with it to the Furnace of Love, You will plunge it for all eternity into the burning Abyss of this Love to which it has offered itself as victim" (Ms B, p. 200 [5vº]). Because in the offering of herself as a "victim of holocaust to Merciful Love" on Trinity Sunday, June 9, 1895, Sr. Thérèse offered herself to the fire of Love.[6]

In fact, "the Living Flame of Love" had fallen upon her. On Friday, June 14, 1895,[7] at the beginning of the Way of the Cross that Thérèse had begun to make alone in the midst of the Carmelite community, her heart was aflame.

Immediately afterwards she spoke to her prioress, Mother Agnès of Jesus, about this extraordinary event. But the latter remained distrustful about everything extraordinary and didn't want to pay any attention.[8] She testified in the Bishop's Process: "In 1895 when I was prioress, she spoke to me about a grace that she called a 'wound of love.' At that time God allowed — undoubtedly to test her — that I didn't pay any attention to what she said. I apparently didn't even believe her and told her so. But in thinking about what she had said to me, I asked myself how I could have doubted her statement for one moment. However I didn't talk to her anymore about it until her final illness. Then (1897) I wanted to make her repeat in the infirmary what she had said to me in 1895 about this wound of love" (PO, 175).

---

[5] Cf. St. Catherine of Siena: "Eternal Trinity, you are fire!" (*Dialogues sur la Providence* [Dialogues on Providence], published by Latina, p. 167).

[6] In a holocaust sacrifice, the victim is entirely consumed by the fire. Cf. R. de Vaux, *Les Institutions de l'Ancien Testament* [Institutions of the Old Testament], Cerf, 1960, bk. II, pp. 292-294.

[7] No certainty for this date, but a strong probability.

[8] Whence the absence of this fact in Manuscript A, dedicated to Mother Agnès of Jesus.

In fact we find under the date of July 7, 1897, this dialogue in her *Last Conversations*: *"I asked her to explain what happened when she made her Act of Oblation to Merciful Love. First she said:* 'Little Mother, I told you this when it took place, but you paid no attention to me.' *This was true; I'd given her the impression that I placed no importance on what she was saying.* 'Well, I was beginning the Way of the Cross; suddenly, I was seized with such a violent love for God that I can't explain it except by saying I felt as though I were totally plunged into fire. Oh! What fire and what sweetness at one and the same time! I was on fire with love, and I felt that one minute more, one second more, and I wouldn't be able to sustain this ardor without dying. I understood, then, what the saints were saying about these states which they experienced so often. As for me, I experienced it only once and for one single instant, falling back immediately into my habitual state of dryness" (CJ 7.7.2 [HLC p. 77]).[9]

Had not Sr. Thérèse wished that the fire of heaven would consume her?: "Consume Your holocaust with the fire of Your Divine Love!" (Ms A, p. 181 [84r°]). It is a "consuming and transforming fire," because "love quickly consumes *everything* that can be displeasing to Jesus" (Ms A, p. 179 [83r°]).

She wrote in September 1896: "O luminous Beacon of love, I know how to reach You, I have found the secret of possessing Your flame" (Ms B, p. 195 [3v°]).

What is this grace, then, that is too often unnoticed by commentators? Because Thérèse habitually lived an ordinary life, we declare too quickly that she didn't receive extraordinary graces. She herself acknowledged that after this wound to her heart she fell back into her "habitual dryness." Too often, we don't know how to interpret this exceptional event.

It wasn't Mother Agnès of Jesus who made the comparison to "the saints who so often experienced" these states. On the contrary, she preferred to ignore them, as she testified in the Bishop's Pro-

---

[9]   Cf. an allusion by Thérèse in her poem: "You put this Fire of Heaven into my soul" (PN 24.17 [*Poetry*, p. 127]).

cess. It is Thérèse herself who evoked these saints, beginning with the "parents" of Carmel, St. Teresa of Avila and St. John of the Cross.

Now Thérèse's text that speaks of "fire," of sweetness and burning, of the impression of dying imminently, calls to mind the transverberation of their Mother, St. Teresa of Avila. There is certainly no angel in the account of the French Carmelite, but the Spanish Carmelite "is completely set on fire by a great love for God," thanks to the shaft[10] that has "a little bit of fire" at its tip. Teresa speaks of "sweetness and pain" (Teresa of Avila, *Life*, XXIX, 13). Note that a statue of the Transverberation of Teresa of Avila had been standing in front of the infirmary in the Carmel since 1882 (cf. VTL, 45, p. 210).

What is all this about? The answer is given to us by St. John of the Cross, who accompanied Sr. Teresa of Jesus on her journey: "Few persons have reached these heights. Some have, however, especially those whose virtue and spirit were to be diffused among their children. With respect to the first fruits of the spirit, God accords to founders wealth and value commensurate with the greater or lesser following they will have in their doctrine and spirituality" (F, 2.12 [K-RJ, p. 662]; cf. p. 172 in Thérèse's edition; Œ/J, p. 1117).

I owe to Fr. Marie-Eugène of the Child Jesus the discovery of the meaning of this event in Thérèse's life in 1895. He comments: "At the fourth station of her Way of the Cross,[11] she receives a wound of love that elevates her for sure (she was probably already there) to the transforming union, which is a wound of spiritual motherhood that we can probably compare to the transverberation of St. Teresa (of Avila) and which will give her the mission of disseminating her knowledge of God. She will therefore take this knowledge of Love

---

[10] It isn't by chance that a shaft is to be found in the coat of arms painted by Thérèse at the end of her first manuscript. She comments: "Thérèse chose this blessed spot (Carmel) to present the *flaming dart* of love that was to merit for her the palm of martyrdom until she could truly shed her blood for *Him whom she loves*" (Ms A, p. 278 [85v°]). The ICS 3rd edition has the image and interpretation of the coat of arms that Thérèse had created).

[11] Only Fr. Marie-Eugène of the Child Jesus provides this point. He was making it about the Carmel of Lisieux (oral communication).

as her departure point in order to transmit her doctrine of spiritual childhood."[12]

In *Je veux voir Dieu*, Fr. Marie-Eugène will comment on the Transverberation of Teresa of Avila by means of a text of St. John of the Cross in *The Living Flame* (sta. 2), which we have quoted.[13] And a little further on, Fr. Marie-Eugène quotes Thérèse of Lisieux. In fact how can we forget the extraordinary number of her disciples and the nearly 50 religious communities that have taken her as their foundress?[14]

Thus did the fire of heaven fall on the heart of Thérèse in response to her offering. The holocaust — according to its very definition — was entirely consumed. This theme of fire was going to become more and more present in her life. The entire end of Manuscript A, which contains in detail the happy consequences of her Act of Oblation, evokes water and fire and, without doubt, an allusion to the "wound of Love."[15]

Being transformed in the living flame of love, Sr. Thérèse wanted to communicate this fire to everybody around her and to the whole world. "This is my prayer. I ask Jesus to draw me into the flames of His love, to unite me so closely to Him that He live and act in me. I feel that the more the fire of love burns within my heart, the more I shall say: 'Draw me,' the more also the souls who will approach me (poor little piece of iron, useless if I withdraw from the divine furnace), the more these souls *will run swiftly in the odor of the ointments of their Beloved*" (Ms C, p. 257 [36r°]).

It is amazing to note how often the theme of fire, of flame, is repeated in the *Poems*, especially after 1895.[16]

---

[12] *Retraite sacerdotale* [Priestly Retreat] at Notre-Dame de Vie, 1962, p. 163.

[13] P. 662. Cf. S. Fumet, *Mikaël. Qui est comme Dieu?* [Michael: Who is like God?] Cerf, 1954, p. 179.

[14] Their Rules of life and their constitutions are inspired by the spirituality of Thérèse. Active congregations comprise the immense majority.

[15] [Ms A, p. 181 (84r°)]; cf. Œ/T, p. 1273, note 415.

[16] Thérèse had read the meditation by Rev. Fr. Tissot given at Paray-le-Monial on 10/15/1890, which Céline had heard while on pilgrimage. She took some notes: "Love is such a divine blaze! (…) Cast this weakness into the Heart of Jesus; scarcely is she within this burning furnace when she is already consumed…" Read this text in VT 79, pp. 224-228.

The Spirit of Love sets me aflame with his fire[17]

Flame of Love, consume me unceasingly[18]

Deign to set me aflame with your fire.[19]

At her voice, my delighted soul
Is set aflame with the fire of Love.[20]

Remember the ever gentle Flame
Which you wanted to enkindle in hearts.
You put this Fire of Heaven in my soul.
I also want to spread its intense heat.
One weak spark, O mystery of life,
Is enough to light a huge fire.[21]

That I want, o my God,
To carry your Fire far and wide.
　　Remember.[22]

And the fire of love which consumes my soul
　　Shall never go out!...[23]

Once the blessed Trinity,
Gazing upon your soul,
Marked you with his Flame
And revealed his beauty to you. (...)

Your heart was all inflamed
At this blessed word.
You gave life for life
To Jesus your Beloved.

---

[17] PN 17.2 [*Poetry*, p. 89].

[18] PN 17.14 [*Poetry*, p. 92].

[19] PN 20.6 [*Poetry*, p. 110].

[20] PN 22.12 [*Poetry*, p. 115].

[21] Book II, p. 380 of Thérèse's edition. Cf. ŒJ, p. 1636. "One single spark can enkindle an immense blaze," St. John of the Cross, Maxim 157 (in a completely different context).

[22] PN 24.17 [*Poetry*, p. 127].

[23] PN 26.9 [*Poetry*, p. 138].

Now, happy victim
Who sacrifice yourself to Love,
Taste the joy, the intimate peace,
Of sacrificing yourself each day.

Your soul longs for Love.
That is your shining star.
Love will be your martyrdom,
Love will open the Heavens for you.[24]

> Your voice echoes in my soul.
> I want to resemble you, Lord.
> I crave suffering.
> Your fiery word
>   Consumes my heart!... (...)

I thirst for Love, fulfill my hope.
Lord, make your Divine Fire grow within me.
I thirst for Love, so great is my suffering.
Ah! I would like to fly away to you, my God!...

> Your Love is my only martyrdom.
> The more I feel it burning within me,
> The more my soul desires you...
> Jesus, make me die
>   Of Love for You!!!...[25]

We understand here the connection between the flame of love that burns and the one that can cause death, as Sr. Thérèse had experienced during her Way of the Cross. "I was on fire with love, and I felt that one minute more, one second more, and I wouldn't be able to sustain this ardor without dying" (cf. *supra*, p. 122).

All these poems date from 1895 and 1896. Her letters during these years ran in the same vein. She wrote to Fr. Roulland on June 23, 1896: "I beg you, Reverend Father, ask for me from Jesus, on

---

[24] PN 29.3,10,11,12 [*Poetry*, pp. 145-146].
[25] PN 31, R 2,6, R. 6 [*Poetry*, pp. 150-151].

the day He deigns for the first time to descend from Heaven at your voice,[26] ask Him to set me on fire with His Love so that I may enkindle it in hearts" [27] (LT 189 [GC II, p. 956]).

The apostolic purpose of the flame's transmission is well emphasized. The month prior to this, commenting on a poem by John of the Cross, she had written for Sr. Marie of the Trinity:

> This fire burning in my soul
> Penetrates my heart forever.
> Thus in its delightful flame
> I am being wholly consumed by love!...[28]

If the offering to love has fanned the flame within her, we can't forget that it was already like this since 1894. Thus:

> Your glance inflames me.
> My only love,
> Consume my soul,
> Jesus, forever.
>
> Oh! what a sweet martyrdom.
> I burn with love,
> To you I sigh,
> Jesus, every day!...[29]

And in the "Canticle of Céline" (4/28/1895):

> Drawn to the gentle flame,
> The moth flies and catches on fire.
> So your love draws my soul.
> In it I want to fly,
> To burn!...[30]

---

26 [I.e., at the first Mass of the newly ordained priest — Trans.]

27 [The author's text reads: "...ask Him to set me on fire with His Love so that I can help you afterwards to enkindle this Fire in the hearts of others" — Trans.]

28 PN, 30.3 [*Poetry*, p. 148].

29 PN 15.4 and 10 [*Poetry*, p. 83].

30 PN 18.53 [*Poetry*, p. 102].

The year 1894 and the beginning of 1895 were intensely focused on the memory of Joan of Arc, whose martyrdom of love for Christ was achieved by fire. Thérèse deeply invested herself in the composition of two recreational plays about Joan. She herself played the role of St. Joan of Arc. We know that on the day of the performance of the second play (RP 3), January 21, 1895, the set caught on fire and Thérèse/Joan was encircled by flames!

The play must be read anew in this perspective:

> From this woodpile the flame is set ablaze,
> But more ardently burning is your God's love. (RP 3, 23r°)

* * *

This fire purifies all failings. St. John of the Cross affirms in the *Spiritual Canticle*: "In this wine cellar these herds of imperfections are more easily consumed than are the rust and tarnish of metal consumed by fire."[31]

Thérèse affirms in the *Act of Oblation*: "If through weakness I sometimes fall, may your Divine Glance cleanse my soul immediately, consuming all my imperfections like the fire that transforms everything into itself" (Pri 6 [*Prayers*, p. 54). This offering had great consequences in Thérèse's life: "Ah! since that happy day (June 9, 1895), it seems to me that *Love* penetrates and surrounds me, that at each moment this *Merciful Love* renews me, purifying my soul and leaving no trace of sin within it, and I need have no fear of purgatory. (…) I also know that of the Fire of Love is more sanctifying than is the fire of purgatory" (Ms A, p. 181 [84r°/v°]).[32]

---

[31] F, commentary on sta. 26 (K-RJ, p. 580). Cf. D. Poirot, "Le Feu, intime amour, chez Jean de la Croix," ["Fire, intimate love, for John of the Cross"], *La Vie spirituelle*, num. 712, 1994, pp. 613-625.

[32] Cf. L. Regnault, "La pensée de sainte Thérèse de l'Enfant-Jésus sur le purgatoire" ["St. Thérèse of the Child Jesus, about purgatory"], VT 101, January-March 1986, pp. 21-29.

She wrote in the same vein to Fr. Bellière two years later: "When we cast our faults with entire filial confidence into the devouring fire of love, how would these not be consumed beyond return?"[33] One of her last words ran in the same vein: "Really tell them, Mother, that if I had committed all possible crimes, I would always have the same confidence; I feel that this whole multitude of offenses would be like a drop of water thrown into a fiery furnace."[34]

We notice that Thérèse never used the symbol of the log (an image used by St. John of the Cross) that is consumed in the fire in order to be purified. She substitutes for it the image of the scrap of iron that "desires to be identified with the fire in such a way that the fire (may) penetrate and drink it up with its burning substance and seem to become one with it" (Ms C, p. 257 [35v°/36r°]).

This is the text of St. John of the Cross:

> *This flame of love is the spirit of its Bridegroom, who is the Holy Spirit. The soul feels him within itself not only as a fire that has consumed and transformed it but as a fire that burns and flares within it, as I mentioned. (...) Such is the activity of the Holy Spirit in the soul transformed in love: the interior acts he produces shoot up flames for they are acts of enflamed love, in which the will of the soul united with that flame, made one with it, loves most sublimely.*[35]

The whole work of St. John of the Cross tends to show that the soul attains a kind of equality with God: "In calling him 'brother,' [the bride] indicates the equality of love between the two in the betrothal before this state (of spiritual marriage) is reached"; "…she asks who will give her the Beloved as her brother (which would both signify equality and produce it)" (C, commentary on stanzas 22 and 24 [K-RJ, pp. 562 and 567]).

---

[33] LT 247 (GC II, pp. 1133-1134).
[34] CJ 7.11.6 [HLC, p. 89]; cf. the final manuscript C (pp. 205ff.).
[35] F, commentary on 1. 3, [K-RJ, p. 641]; cf. p. 130 of Thérèse's edition.

Thérèse also uses the word "brother":

> I must have a God who takes on my nature
> And becomes my brother and is able to suffer!
> (PN 23.4 [*Poetry*, p. 119])

> For you, my Divine Little Brother,
> I'm happy to suffer...   (PN 45.6 [*Poetry*, p. 186])

Spiritual marriage works in this manner: "The union wrought between the two natures and the communication of the divine to the human in this state is such that even though neither changes its being, both appear to be God"[36] (C, commentary on sta. 22, p. 561).

In her notebook, Céline had copied maxim 69 of St. John of the Cross, of which we emphasize the ending:

> *God desires to make gods of us, through participation in what he is himself by nature, just as the fire converts everything into fire.*[37]

In the famous letter 197 of September 17, 1896, Thérèse had written to her sister Marie of the Sacred Heart: "Oh, dear Sister, I beg you, understand your little girl, understand that to love Jesus, to be His *victim of love*, the weaker one is, without desires or virtues, the more suited one is for the workings of this consuming and transforming Love"[38] [GC II, p. 999].

And she concludes her last manuscript with these lines: "This is my prayer. I ask Jesus to draw me into the flames of His love, to

---

[36] As early as March 12, 1889, we read in a letter from Thérèse to Céline: "...after having drunk at the fountain of all sorrows, we shall be deified at the very fountain of all joys" (LT 85 [GC I, p. 546]). *To be deified* is an expression used only once in her writings. She had read in Arminjon (7th conference which had made a great impression on her): "They themselves become Gods" (*Fin du monde présent et Mystères de la vie future* [End of the present world and Mysteries of the future life], published by OCL, 1970, p. 207); [cf. GC I, note 4, p. 547 — Trans.]

[37] Pri 6, note 37-38 (*Prayers*, p. 72).

[38] Thérèse uses the verb *consommer* ("to use completely") only in Pri 12 and LT 245. She often prefers *consumer* ("to burn"), relating to the image of the fire: Ms A, p. 181 (84r°); Pri 6 [*Prayers*, p. 54]; cf. note 10 to Pri 16, NEC, p. 605.

unite me so closely to Him that he live and act in me" (Ms C, p. 257 [36r°]).

Paul Claudel, the great poet who converted the same day as Thérèse (December 25, 1886), can conclude this first part with this lyrical passage that seems to us even truer today:

> Your sacrifice is pleasing, Mademoiselle Martin! This pyre, completely united with its victim, which is your body and soul, God himself has swooped down upon as in the days of Elijah, to set fire to it. O, holy Virgin, it isn't the oil missing from the lamp of which the Canticle speaks — *lampades ignis atque flammarum* ["The flash of it is a flash of fire" (Sg 8:6)] — it is your Spouse Himself who is responsible for setting the fire! "I have come to bring fire to the earth" (yes, yes, to this same clay you inherited from Adam), "and how I wish it were blazing already!" [Lk 12:49] Burn, then, Thérèse! Burn, flame fed by your own breath! Burn black, burn clear, holocaust, until I have decomposed you in flesh and spirit! Burn, candle! What does she mean, this little girl burning like a Pentecost, asking me that My will be done, as if that must not be started by her; My will, as if there were not hers first to bring fire to Mine? As if, even the soul already all prepared, there remained no body through which complete consumption can take place? *Who will devour like I do?* says the fire.[39]

"Death of love"

Mother Agnès of Jesus reports in her *Last Conversations*: "In the evening she recalled for me St. John of the Cross's words: "'Tear through the veil of this sweet encounter!' I've always applied these words to the death of love that I desire. Love will not wear out the veil of my life; it will tear it suddenly'" (CJ 7.27.5 [HLC, p. 113]).[40]

---

[39] *Trois figures saintes pour le temps actuel* [Three saints for our times], published by Amiot-Dumont, 1953, pp. 82-83.

[40] F, 1. 6, p. 150 in Thérèse's edition; (K-RJ, p. 578).

Five weeks later, the patient will again say: "…Oh! yes, I desire Heaven! 'Tear the veil of this sweet encounter,' Oh my God!" (CJ 9.2.8 [HLC, p. 181]).

From 1895 on, Thérèse often expressed this desire "to die of love." It is in the tradition of Carmel.[41] Let us not forget that the poem *Living on Love* was composed spontaneously:

> I want to sing on leaving this world:
> "I'm dying of Love!"
> (…)
> Flame of Love, consume me unceasingly.
> Life of an instant, your burden is so heavy to me!
> Divine Jesus, make my dream come true:
> To die of Love!
> Dying of Love is what I hope for (…)
> I want to be set on fire with his Love…
>   (PN 17.13-15 [*Poetry*, p. 92])

In the *Song of Céline* (4/28/1895):

> O Jesus! may I die one day
>   Of Love!…   (PN 18.52 [*Poetry*, p. 102])

Again in 1895, Joan of Arc — played by Thérèse — proclaims before the pyre:

> To die for your love, I want nothing more…   (RP 3.21r°)

In a final letter of June 6, 1897, to her novice Sr. Marie of the Trinity, Thérèse expressed this wish: "I do not count on the illness, it is too slow a leader. *I count only* on *love*. Ask Good Jesus that all the prayers being offered for me may serve to increase the Fire which must consume me…" (LT 242 [CG II, p. 1121]). Three days later,

---

[41] In the case of St. Teresa of Avila, cf. E. Renault, O.C.D., *Le Désire de mourir chez Thérèse d'Avila* [Teresa of Avila, the desire to die], in *Sainte Thérèse d'Avila*, Colloque Notre-Dame de Vie, 1982, pp. 183-193.

she confided anew to Mother Marie de Gonzague her trial against faith. She said at the end: "It seems to me now that nothing could prevent me from flying away, for I no longer have any great desires except that of loving to the point of dying of love (June 9)" (Ms C, p. 214 [7vº]).

In the infirmary during the night of July 12, the patient again composed a verse to prepare herself for Holy Communion:

> You who know my extreme littleness,
> You aren't afraid to lower yourself to me!
> Come into my heart, O white Host that I love,
> Come into my heart, it longs for you!
> Ah! I wish that your goodness
> Would let me die of love after this favor.
> Jesus! Hear the cry of my affection.
> Come into my heart! (PS 8 [*Poetry*, p. 233])

With a high and beautiful voice, Sr. Marie of the Eucharist sang this stanza before Thérèse's communion in the infirmary on July 16. After communion she sang stanza 14 from *Living on Love,* which we have quoted.[42] This desire to die of love, so often emphasized, certainly owes a lot to St. John of the Cross. People around Thérèse knew it.

As for Thérèse, she had *The Living Flame of Love* at her bedside, and marked some little crosses in the text in pencil in order to respond to a wish of Mother Agnès: "When I was speaking to her about her desire to die of love, asking her how we would know that she had loved God 'to the point of dying of love,' she marked in the book with a little penciled cross this passage by the same author touching on the souls consumed in perfect Love: 'They die in wonderful transports and from delectable assaults until Love delivers them,' etc." (NPPA; cf. DE, pp. 492-493 [HLC p. 148]).

Obviously it is necessary to read attentively these three pas-

---

[42] Cf. the account of this celebration written by Thérèse to the Guérins, LT 255 [CG II, p. 1146].

sages from *The Living Flame of Love* emphasized by the sick Thérèse. They are as follows (cf. Œ/J, pp. 1106-1109):

- *Page 152:* "The death of these souls is accompanied by a sweetness and a marvelous mellowness that far surpass everything they had tasted during their entire spiritual life. They die amid wonderful transports and from delectable assaults until Love delivers them, like the swan whose song is most melodious at the point of death. This is what David said, that *the death of the just is precious in the sight of God* (Ps 116:15). For at such a time the rivers of love escape from the soul, and are about to lose themselves in the ocean of divine love. There they are so great and powerful that they seem to be seas already. There the beginning and the end, the first and the last unite together (Rv 22:13), to accompany the just on his way to his kingdom; and *one hears resound from the ends of the world,* according to the word of Isaiah, *the praises that are the glory of the just* (Is 24:16)."

- *Page 156:* "And so, the soul who is prepared can perform more acts, and acts of much greater intensity, in a few moments than the soul who is not prepared can perform in a much longer time."

- *Pp. 157-158:* "And so, this soul wishes not to wait for the natural end of her life, because the force of her love and the dispositions she sees in herself make her desire, undoubtedly with resignation to God's will, to dash herself to pieces under the violent and supernatural impulse of love. She knows very well that God's custom is to take away these souls before their time, in order to enrich them with his good things and to remove them from the evils of this world. He consumes them in perfection in a very short time, and as the Wise Man says, gives them, thanks to this love, what they might have gained only with long effort. *As the just man pleased God, God has loved him; and God has transferred him from among the sinners with whom he lived. He has taken him away, from fear lest his spirit be corrupted by harm and lest false appearances seduce his soul... Although he lived a short time, he has fulfilled the course of a long life, for his soul was pleasing to God. This is why God hastened to take him out from the midst of unrighteousness* (Ws 4:10,11,13,14). It is therefore of the highest importance that the soul practice love very much so that, being consumed rapidly, she may be scarcely retained here on earth but swiftly reach the vision of her God face to face."

The autobiographical allusion is unmistakable. Contrary to what certain Carmelites in that community were thinking and saying, a short life can live love to a white-hot degree. We know Thérèse's predilection for the saints who died young (and as martyrs): the Holy Innocents, Cecilia, Agnes, Joan of Arc, Aloysius Gonzaga, Théophane Venard, Stanislas Kostka.... All were rapidly immolated — and consumed.[43] In her play about *Joan of Arc accomplishing her mission* (RP 3), Thérèse adds the passage from the book of Wisdom (4:7-17) about the premature death of the just.

The deciphering of a Bristol bookmark containing some short references to other readings of Thérèse, is not easy. We will return to it in a study in the Appendix (p. 156).

* * *

Throughout the physical suffering of tuberculosis and the moral and spiritual sufferings of the trial of faith, what became of the desire "to die of love"?

The abrupt ups and downs of the illness — sometimes Thérèse was close to death, sometimes she was better — oriented her towards a holy "indifference," to use the words of St. Ignatius Loyola. "After all, it's the same to me whether I live or die" (CJ 5.15.7 [HLC, p. 45]). "But deep down, I am completely resigned to living, or dying, or getting well and going to Cochin China,[44] if God so wills" (CJ

---

[43] [*Consumés* — and *consommés*; cf. p. 43, note 5; p. 130, note 38 — Trans.]

[44] The eventuality of Sr. Thérèse's departure for Carmel in Saigon (founded by the Lisieux Carmel in 1861), was seriously envisioned (cf. Ms C, p. 217 [9rº/10vº]; LT 221 [GC II, p. 1071]; CJ 9.2.5 [HLC, p. 180]).

5.21-26.2 [HLC, p. 49]). "I don't want to die more than to live; that is, if I had the choice, I would prefer to die. But since it's God who makes the choices for me, I prefer what He wills. It's what He does that I love" (CJ 5.27.4 [HLC, pp. 50-51]).

She had written in February of 1895:

> Lord, I'm willing to live a long time more,
> If that is your desire.
> I'd like to follow you to Heaven
> If that would make you happy.
> Love, that fire from the Homeland,
> Never ceases to consume me.
> What do life and death matter to me?
> Jesus, my joy, it's to love you!
>
> (PN 45.7 [*Poetry*, p. 186])

On May 31, 1897, she wrote a song entitled "Abandonment Is the Sweet Fruit of Love" (PN 52 [*Poetry*, p. 205]).

At her bedside, the Martin sisters, ever present — especially Mother Agnès of Jesus — and knowing the texts of *The Living Flame* about "the death of love," were awaiting the realization of these pages. This impatience, sometimes indiscreet and tiring for the sick nun, seems a remedy for their own pain. It is revealing to read Sr. Geneviève's lines to Br. Siméon in Rome: "Her illness is love. She suffers nothing other than to die of love as she so much desired."[45] It is true that Sr. Thérèse expressed this desire a great many times.

In her famous poem from February 1895, "*Living on Love*" [*Poetry*, p. 92], she expressed this hope for the first time:[46]

> Dying of Love is a truly sweet martyrdom,
> And that is the one I wish to suffer.

---

[45] DE, pp. 680-681.

[46] But in her theater play of January 1895, she had Joan of Arc, "her dear sister" (Ms B, p. 139 [3r°]), say: "To die for your love, I want nothing else / I desire to die to begin to live / I desire to die to unite myself to Jesus" (RP 3, 21r°).

O, Cherubim! Tune your lyre,
For I sense my exile is about to end!…
Flame of Love, consume me unceasingly.
Life of an instant, your burden is so heavy to me!
Divine Jesus, make my dream come true:
    To Die of Love!…

Dying of Love is what I hope for.
When I shall see my bonds broken,
My God will be my Great Reward.
I don't desire to possess other goods.
I want to be set on fire with his Love.
I want to see Him, to unite myself to Him forever.
That is my Heaven!… that is my destiny:
    Living on Love!!! …. (PN 17.15-16 [*Poetry*, p. 92])

We obviously notice how much the death of love is connected
with the consuming fire of divine Love. In the following poem, we
note:

O, Jesus! may I die one day
    Of Love!…   (PN 18.52 [*Poetry*, p. 102])

In October 1895, after the Oblation to Merciful Love on June
9 ("may I thus become a Martyr of your Love… May this martyrdom finally make me die…" Pri 6 [*Poetry*, p. 55]), the long song *Jesus,
My Beloved, Remember!* is explicit:

Remember, Jesus, Word of Life,
How you loved me and even died for me.
I also want to love you to folly.
I also want to live and die for You.
You know, O my God! all that I desire
Is to make you loved and one day be a martyr.
I want to die of Love.
Lord, my desire,
    Remember.   (PN 24.26 [*Poetry*, p. 129])

The conclusion of *Canticle of Sister Marie of the Trinity and of the Holy Face* remains without equal:

> Your Love is my only martyrdom.
> The more I feel it burning in me,
> The more my soul desires you…
>   Jesus, make me die
>   Of Love for You!!!…   (PN 31, R.6. [*Poetry*, p. 151])

We notice the permanent link between the fire of Trinitarian Love, death and martyrdom of love. At the bedside of the ill Thérèse, the Martin sisters mentioned the texts by St. John. Thus, Mother Agnès of Jesus: "I was recalling for her what St. John of the Cross said about the death of those who were consumed in love."[47] Thérèse's answer had disconcerted her sister at first. "She sighed and said: *'I shall have to say that "joy and transports" are at the bottom of my heart. But it wouldn't be so encouraging to souls if they didn't believe I suffered very much.'* I said: 'How I sense your agony! And yet it's a month ago that you were saying such beautiful things about the death of love.' *'What I was saying then, I would say right now'*" (CJ 8.15.1 [HLC, p. 148]).

Sr. Thérèse wanted to remain on the firm ground of faith, being a good disciple of the Spanish Carmelite: "Don't be astonished if I don't appear to you after my death, and if you see nothing extraordinary as a sign of my happiness.[48] You will remember that it's 'my little way' not to desire to see anything" (CJ 6.4.1 [HLC, p. 55]). She adds: "Don't be troubled, little sisters, if I suffer very much and if you see in me, as I've already said, no sign of happiness at the moment of my death. Our Lord really died as Victim of Love, and you see what His agony was!… All this says nothing" [p. 56].

Thus, since the month of June, Thérèse, gazing at Jesus — we know that she very often held her crucifix in her hand — recognized

---

[47] Cf. pp. 136 ff. (above). F, 1.6. Passage marked by Thérèse with a penciled cross (DE, p. 492).

[48] In fact, her posthumous life since 1899 will be an extraordinary succession of "signs," including many apparitions.

the "death of love" by the signs that may accompany it. So she distanced herself from the texts of *The Living Flame*. Only one argument, taken from the Gospels, seemed to her irrefutable: the death of Jesus himself. Such was his death of love on Calvary; she wanted nothing else, faithful to the short prayer that she always carried on her heart: "Make me resemble You, Jesus!" (Pri 11 [*Prayers*, p. 89]).

From whence this important affirmation comes in July: "Our Lord died on the Cross in agony, and yet this is the most beautiful death of love. This is the only one that was seen; no one saw that of the Blessed Virgin. To die of love is not to die in transports. I tell you frankly, it seems to me that this is what I am experiencing" (CJ 7.4.2 [HLC, p. 73]).

This is a major disclosure that throws brilliant light on the passion of Sr. Thérèse. As baffling as it may be to the people around her and to posterity, it finds its ultimate meaning in the patient's intense love for Jesus and his "glorious Cross" (Ms B, p. 193 [3r°]).

The terrible development of her illness, the dark night of faith (scarcely mentioned in her *Last Conversations* and known only to Mother Marie de Gonzague, less even by Mother Agnès of Jesus), seemed to contradict, little by little, the hopes concerning a "beautiful" death of love. The people around her questioned themselves. Did this doubt not come to Thérèse herself during dark moments? Was she deceived? For inner voices suggested to her that death will bring her only "nothingness" (Ms C, p. 213 [6v°]). Didn't she mention several times the temptation to suicide?[49]

She never let go of her crucifix and contemplated it very often. The most beautiful death of love is that of the Crucified who died "crying out in a great voice" (Mt 27:50) after having prayed Psalm 22[21]: "My God, my God, why have you forsaken me?" Sr. Thérèse no longer thought that something had to look like what it *is*: "It is not the pain it appears to be [*to die of love*], provided it is really it!" (CJ 7.14.4 [HLC, p. 97]).

---

[49] CJ 9.22.6 [HLC, p. 196] and Sr. Marie of the Trinity, PO 47,2. During some bad nights, the Devil sought to drive her to despair: CJ 8.25.6 [HLC, p. 168]; 9.11.5 and 6 [p. 188]; 9.29.3 [pp. 201-202].

One more time they suggested to her the possibility of a somewhat spectacular "beautiful death": to die on the feast of Our Lady
of Mount Carmel, after Holy Communion. That would look so good
in her obituary, and souls would be so edified by it! Thérèse pro-
tested: "Oh, that wouldn't resemble my little way. Would you want
me to leave this little way, then, in order to die? Dying after receiving Holy Communion would be too beautiful for me; little souls
couldn't imitate this" (CJ 7.15.1 [HLC, p. 98]).

Thus Thérèse's death of love remains in profound harmony
with her little way. She must stay in the dark night of faith and hope.
But is this not to remain faithful to the teachings of St. John of the
Cross, the Doctor of the Faith, which we heard in our Second Chapter? We must not forget that he himself describes Christ's death on
the cross in shocking relief, in perfect accord with the famous draw-
ing he has left us of the tormented expression of the Crucified:

> …at the moment of his death he was certainly annihilated in
> his soul, without any consolation or relief, since the Father
> had left him that way in innermost aridity in the lower part
> [his human nature]. He was thereby compelled to cry out *My
> God, my God, why have you forsaken me?'* (Mt 27:46). This was
> the most extreme abandonment, sensitively, that he had suf-
> fered in his life. And by it he accomplished the most marvel-
> ous work of his whole life, surpassing all the works and deeds
> and miracles that he had ever performed on earth or in heaven
> (…) that those who are truly spiritual might understand the
> mystery of the door and way (which is Christ), leading to
> union with God, and that they might realize that their union
> with God and the greatness of the work they accomplish will
> be measured by their annihilation of themselves for God in
> the sensory and spiritual parts of their souls. When they are
> reduced to nothing, the highest degree of humility, the spiri-
> tual union between their souls and God, will be an accom-
> plished fact. This union is the most noble and sublime state
> attainable in this life. The journey, then, does not consist in
> consolations, delights and spiritual feelings, but in the living

death of the cross, sensory and spiritual, exterior and interior
(A, II. 7.11 [K-RJ, pp. 172]).

How could we forget the poem of *The Shepherd (Song of Christ and the soul)* and its last stanza:

> Time passes. Finally he climbed
> Up a tree, his arms wide open.
> Look at him dead, he hangs suspended,
> His heart, alas, torn apart by love.[50]

Furthermore, the death of love of John of the Cross, the one who wanted "to suffer and be despised," did conform to that of his Beloved Master. This was the description by Fr. Marie-Eugène of the Child Jesus in three days of prayer at the Lisieux Carmel in 1927: "Jesus-Crucified led him [John of the Cross] into the depth of his sufferings and imprinted its painful traces on his face. Wounds invaded his whole body and there was no longer one healthy limb in him. No more physical strength, no more beauty. He is a 'man of sorrows,' 'the least of men,' 'the least of religious.' The prior of the convent of Ubeda barely likes him. Does he not seem struck down by God himself since those who are the authentic instruments of God's justice attack him? Inner desolation and abandonment increase the waves of suffering. When Fr. Antoine comes, the patient will ask him to excuse him because he is overwhelmed by suffering. This is the black hole. 'My God, my God, why have you forsaken me?'"[51]

All of this is confirmed and detailed in the historic account of the Spanish Carmelite's death. We must read these dramatic pages.[52] Let us summarize them.

Fr. Francisco Crisostomo, the prior, received him inhospita-

---

[50] Œ/J, p. 147.

[51] 3ʳᵈ Conference: *"Victime d'Amour"* [Victim of Love]. Cf. *Jean de la Croix, Présence de lumière* [John of the Cross, Presence of light], p. 137.

[52] J.V. Rodriguez, *Dieu parle dans la nuit* [God speaks in the night], pp. 360-369. This is corroborated by Fr. Crisogono de Jesús, *Jean de la Croix, sa vie* [John of the Cross, his life], Cerf, 1982, pp. 366-387.

bly into the convent of Ubeda. He complained about the expenses caused by the patient, showed himself jealous of him, relieved the nursing brother of his duties, and spread slanders about Br. John's way of living. The latter's physical sufferings were not less terrible: he had an abscess on his thigh that spread to the ankle. With a pair of scissors the doctor made an incision on him eight inches long! On his back an abscess larger than a fist was discharging pus. "His sufferings were excruciating and increased every day" (p. 365). John could no longer eat.

The nursing brother admired his extraordinary patience, the continual offering of his sufferings to God, his constant remembrance of Christ's sufferings. He never let go of his crucifix. On December 14, 1591, at midnight, his last words were those of Christ: "Into your hands, Lord, I commend my spirit." Thus was the life of Br. John completed who had gone to sing night prayer in heaven.

Sr. Teresa Benedicta of the Cross (Edith Stein) wrote in 1941, before dying in Auschwitz: "The summit of Golgotha was reached."[53]

* * *

With Fr. Marie-Eugène of the Child Jesus, we conclude this chapter about the death of love in the living flame: "So, for Thérèse of the Child Jesus, come to Carmel to pray for sinners and priests, the last phase of transforming love before the vision of heaven was certainly a burning, consuming love. But the sweetness that John of the Cross indicates would be hidden under the redemptive suffering of sin that the Saint bore and which accomplished in her Christ's death on the Cross that she had desired."[54]

---

[53] *La science de la Croix* [The science of the Cross], 1957, published by Nauwelaerts, p. 24.

[54] *Je veux voir Dieu* [I want to see God], p. 937. Fr. André Combes has studied the relationship between the death from love according to St. John of the Cross and Thérèse of Lisieux in his *Introduction à la spiritualité de sainte Thérèse de l'Enfant-Jésus* [Introduction to the spirituality of St. Thérèse of the Child Jesus], Vrin, 1948, pp. 464-476. He remarks that the dependence is "certain" regarding the Spanish Carmelite, always emphasizing that Thérèse "keeps all her originality" (p. 465). He affirms that there is a clearly

We can assess what path the 15-year-old postulant took in order to arrive there, only nine years later. Did she not say on the day of her death: "...All my little desires have been realized.... Now this great one (*to die of love*) has to be!" (CJ 9.30).[55] Is she not one of those souls of whom St. John of the Cross speaks, who having ardently desired martyrdom, die "in bed" (CJ 8.4.7 [HLC, p. 132]) and who are nevertheless "martyrs of love":

> Here is another example: A soul has intense desires to be a martyr. God answers, 'You shall be a martyr' and bestows deep interior consolation and confidence in the truth of this promise. Regardless of the promise, this person in the end does not die a martyr: yet the promise will have been true. Why, then, was there no fulfillment of the promise? Because it will be fulfilled in its chief, essential meaning: the bestowal of the essential love and reward of a martyr. God truly grants the soul what it formerly desired and what he promised it because the formal desire of the soul was not a manner of death but the service of God through martyrdom and the exercise of a martyr's love for him. Death through martyrdom in itself is of no value without this love, and God bestows martyrdom's love and reward perfectly by other means. Even though the soul does not die a martyr, it is profoundly satisfied since God has fulfilled its desire (A, II, 19. 13 [K-RJ, p. 219]).

He was John *of the Cross*, she was Thérèse *of the Holy Face*, brother and sister.

---

conscious difference between the two saints: "Leaving to St. John of the Cross the responsibility and privilege of his flamboyant descriptions, Thérèse searches much higher for the model to which every Christian must conform, the doctrine that teaches the pure truth without any danger of illusion. Her model is Christ on the Cross. Her doctrine is the extreme sobriety or the divine silence of the Gospels about the Crucified's state of soul. Unable to doubt that He who is substantially Love doesn't die of Love, it is his death that Thérèse contemplates. (...) It is to this very death that she asks for the grace to conform herself." A. Combes speaks of a "return to the Gospel" (pp. 468-469). We reach the same conclusions, but having described the death of St. John of the Cross, we have to modify what Combes calls "divergence."

[55] DE, p. 391, Œ/J, p. 1146 [This quote in not found in HLC — Trans.].

CONCLUSION

"Jesus will come to look for us, and however far
we may be, He will transform us
in flames of love...."

LT 197 (GC II, p. 999)

T HE MOST FAMOUS DAUGHTER OF ST. JOHN OF the Cross" — that is how Fr. Marie-Eugène of the Child Jesus called Thérèse.[1]

Without having exhaustively treated the subject of the Spanish Father's influence on the young Norman Carmelite, we think we have shown that it cannot be restricted to 1890-1891. To limit the influence to those two years would be an error. Inspired by "the Saint of Love and Faith" since her adolescence, Thérèse never abandoned him. His influence would be felt until the very pangs of her last agony. That is our essential conclusion, grounded on the texts and testimonies.

Our predecessors did not have at their disposal all the documents that we have since the labors of the New Centenary Edition, which have taken almost forty years. What might have misled the more superficial reader is that the young Carmelite, who was extremely independent, kept practically nothing of John of the Cross's

---

[1]   *Je veux voir Dieu* [I want to see God], p. 698.

terminology. We would seek in vain in her writings and sayings for words like "active night of the senses, passive nights of the spirit, passions and inclinations, purifications...." And we find not at all the famous images of John of the Cross: *the burning log*, etc., nor technical terms like *anagogical act*, etc.

Sr. Thérèse spontaneously understood the essence of St. John of the Cross's message, simplifying it without watering it down. But the historical contexts of both saints were very different. John of the Cross wrote in a context of Spanish Christianity in the XVI century — the Golden Age — addressing himself to people who wanted to seriously engage in the search for God, especially his Carmelite sisters.[2] "Little" Thérèse wrote — without really wanting to, but "out of obedience" — for "a great number of *little* souls" (Ms B, p. 200 [5vº]): for the masses, for the poor, the handicapped in life, the stressed ones of our modern world. Anticipating the texts of Vatican Council II, which call all the baptized to holiness, the young Carmelite wrote in a context of contemporary de-christianization. Her trial of faith and hope placed her at the "table of sinners" (Ms C, p. 212 [6rº]).

Fr. Bernard Bro, O.P. could say that she "democratized the dark night." Sr. Thérèse's "heroism of littleness" is as absolute as the most radical propositions of St. John of the Cross. We can't compare "the little way" to transforming union as if one would overshadow the other; in Christianity there is no second-rate holiness. Not a popular "little Thérèse" versus an elitist and aristocratic "great St. John of the Cross." She is his daughter, in the same lineage of evangelical holiness.

Certainly there are differences between them. He is a theologian, a former student of the University of Salamanca, spiritually in love with the Absolute of God, and an incomparable Spanish poet, one of the greatest of his century. She is a little French girl who left

---

[2] "Besides, my main intention is not to address everyone, but only some of the persons of our holy order of the primitive observance of Mount Carmel..." (Prologue to *The Ascent of Mount Carmel*, K-RJ, p. 118).

grade school at the age of 13 and a half, who received no theological training and whose songs stay consistent with the religious versification of her times. Beyond all aestheticism it remains that we find in both of them the same experience of God, the same expression of an intense spiritual life.

In a different way Georges Bernanos, a profound tributary of Thérèse's spirituality, writes in his somewhat rough style:

> ...this mysterious girl (...) has sewn seed here on earth with her innocent little hands, with her terrible little hands well-skilled in cutting out paper flowers, but also eaten away by chlorine detergents and chilblains, a seed that nothing will stop from germination. (...) I want to keep my distance from all the poetic popularization of St. John of the Cross — the coarseness of my temperament luckily keeps me away from readings that are too enormous for me. If a dictionary of mysticism exists, I wouldn't open it. (...) Let us become children again. (...) Are you capable of rejuvenating the world? A Saint whose lightning career sufficiently shows the tragically urgent character of the message that was entrusted to her, invites you to become children again.[3]

John of the Cross and Thérèse of the Child Jesus and of the Holy Face have been pilgrims of the absolute, each in their own way but, according to an expression of Jacques Maritain, the French Carmelite "put contemplation on the streets."[4] For his part, Fr. Marie-Eugène of the Child Jesus, a fervent disciple of Thérèse, wanted to put contemplation "on the highways and byways."[5]

---

[3] "Let there be no doubt about it, the way of childhood leads to the highest summits of contemplation and transforming union that St. John of the Cross wrote about. She climbed them in peace and joy. The simplicity of the teaching of St. Thérèse of the Child Jesus is the sublimity of doctrine, and the smile that she bestows on everything is the perfection of love" (Fr. Marie-Eugène, *Je veux voir* [I want to see God], p. 847).

[4] *Le Paysan de la Garonne* [The Peasant of the Garonne], pp. 337 and 340. *Carmel*, March 1968, pp. 114-115.

[5] "*Dans les faubourgs, sur les boulevards*" (in the outskirts, on the boulevards — Trans.), *Carmel*, March 1968, p. 115.

Maritain goes on: "This way is the way of the 'poor people,' it is the 'little way' that St. Thérèse of Lisieux was given the responsibility to teach us. It is a kind of shortcut — extremely abrupt, to tell the truth — where all the great things written by St. John of the Cross find themselves divinely simplified and reduced to their very essence but without losing any of their importance."[6]

In turn Raïssa Maritain, his wife, a contemplative living in the world, has written: "The great necessity in our times concerning spiritual life is to put contemplation on the streets. It is appropriate to notice here the importance of the testimony and the mission of St. Thérèse of Lisieux. Truly it is a great way, rather than a 'little way' — and a heroic one — but it rigorously hides its grandeur under an absolute simplicity, itself heroic. And this absolute simplicity makes it par excellence a way open to all who long for perfection, whatever their condition of life may be. St. Thérèse of the Child Jesus has shown that the soul can tend to the perfection of charity by a way in which the great signs that St. John of the Cross and St. Teresa of Avila wrote about do not appear..."[7]

The Carmelite Fr. Lucien of St. Mary, editor and commentator of St. John of the Cross,[8] could write: "What is touching about this marvel is that a 17-year-old child encounters a genius of extraordinary power, discovers him without intellectual stimulation in her secular or religious education, nourishes herself on him almost exclusively for two years,[9] bears his influence but doesn't copy his doctrine.... The more we discover traces of the imprints made by the works of St. John of the Cross, the more we marvel at the autonomy with which she integrates them.... She is in no way a commentator, she is herself."[10]

---

[6] *Op. cit.*, p. 339.

[7] *Liturgie et Contemplation* [Liturgy and Contemplation], Paris, 1959, pp. 77-78.

[8] Fr. Lucien (1906-1981) edited the *Œuvres* [Works] of St. John of the Cross in *la Bibliothèque européenne* [The European Library], DDB, 1959.

[9] Our study has shown that the influence of St. John of the Cross lasted beyond these two years, 1890-1891.

[10] "Thérèse de l'Enfant-Jésus ou l'enfance unie à la maturité ["Thérèse of the Child Jesus or childhood united with maturity"], *La Vie spirituelle*, 1952, book 85, p. 305.

It is true that Sr. Thérèse, free, light, brilliant,[11] inspired by the Holy Spirit, was never a student who took scrupulous notes from her Master's writings. Her reading, with the help of her immense memory, was something quite different, aimed entirely at a single goal: "To love Jesus and to make him loved." Passionately she gathered all the flowers from which to make her honey. She had no scruples about freely interpreting the Spanish Carmelite's thinking. We have seen, besides, that she frankly confirmed this autonomy when answering a question of her novice, Sr. Marie of the Trinity: "'*Where do you get this teaching from?*' God alone has taught me. No book, no theologian taught me, yet I feel at the bottom of my heart that I am in the truth. I received no encouragement from anyone and when the occasion came to open my soul, I was so little understood that I said to God like St. John of the Cross: 'Do not send me any more messengers; they cannot tell me what I must hear'" (C, sta. 6 [K-RJ, p. 74]). Unintentional humor? To affirm her independence, Thérèse quotes John of the Cross and somewhat compares herself to him![12]

The final conclusion of this study belongs to the dying Thérèse. We have already quoted the main saying in the *Last Conversations*, which sets the seal of truth on the route we have followed: "Ah! It is incredible how all my hopes have been fulfilled. When I used to read St. John of the Cross, I begged God to work out in me what he wrote, that is, the same thing as though I were to live to be very old; to consume me rapidly in Love, and *I have been answered!*" (CJ 8.31.9 [HLC, p. 177], emphasis ours). This is an unbeatable conclusion... "Everything is said, right? (…) — Yes!" (CJ 8.19.8 [HCL, p. 155]).

Let us listen one more time to St. John of the Cross who summarizes the thérésian story, a work of the Holy Spirit. "Through this [dark night of] contemplation, God teaches the soul secretly and

---

[11] Cf. J. Guitton, *Le Génie de Thérèse de Lisieux* [The genius of Thérèse of Lisieux], published by OCL-Emmanuel, 1995. And Fr. Marie-Eugène of the Child Jesus, *Under the Torrent of His Love.*

[12] P. Descouvemont, *Thérèse of Lisieux and Marie of the Trinity*, p. 37, n. 66, quoting CRM 103.

instructs it in the perfection of love without its doing anything or understanding how this happens" (N, 2. 5. 1 [K-RJ, p. 401]).

* * *

We do hope, together with innumerable friends of St. Thérèse of Lisieux, to one day see her proclaimed Doctor of the Church[13] like her "Father" was in 1926, and her "Mother" in 1970.[14]

She played a part in the achievement of getting the doctorate for her Master. The universal glory of her canonization (1925) has not been without influence on the glory of St. John of the Cross: "Is not a ray of Thérèse's glory today rising towards her Blessed Father? And is she not the one who dissipated the semidarkness in which he was living for two centuries?"[15]

Would it not be just that the Spanish saint now intercede in favor of his daughter, who prayed that he be proclaimed a Doctor of the Church?[16] We ardently hope so. We are submitting this wish again, shared by hundreds of bishops all over the world and by hundreds of thousands of baptized people, to the judgment and wisdom of the Church, enlightened by the Holy Spirit.

Let us hope that this book, among many others, may contribute to showing the inexhaustible depth of the spiritual theology of St. Thérèse of Lisieux.

---

[13] According to her desire expressed on September 8, 1896: "I feel the *vocation* of… the DOCTOR…" (Ms B, p. 192 [2v°]). The process was opened in 1932 and taken up again in 1990. [On October 19, 1997, Pope John Paul II declared St. Thérèse of the Child Jesus and of the Holy Face to be a Doctor of the Church, a Doctor of Merciful Love — Trans.]

[14] Pope Paul VI declared St. Teresa of Avila a Doctor of the Church in 1970, as well as St. Catherine of Siena.

[15] Fr. Marie-Eugène of the Child Jesus, *Triduum saint Jean de la Croix* [St. John of the Cross Triduum], p. 52.

[16] In 1947, Fr. Philipon, O.P., author of *Sainte Thérèse de Lisieux. "Une vie toute nouvelle"* [St. Thérèse of Lisieux. "A completely new way"], DDB, 1946, wrote to Mother Agnès of Jesus: "This trio has much to say to the modern world. Carmel doesn't have two Doctors, but three" (Archives of the Carmel of Lisieux).

APPENDICES

I. *Statistics*
    Quotations of St. John of the Cross in the writings
    of St. Thérèse of Lisieux.

II. *The Bristol bookmark* in the infirmary, referring us to the
    Spiritual Canticle and *The Living Flame of Love.*

III. *Some opinions* concerning the influence of St. John of the
     Cross on St. Thérèse of Lisieux.

I. *Statistics*

Quotations of St. John of the Cross in the writings of St. Thérèse.

One can go back to pages 1554-1556 in the single volume of the *Collected Works* of St. Thérèse (Cerf-DDB), which give tables and information on the notes referring to the Spanish Carmelite.

In total, there are about 100 quotations.
In Ms A: 19
In Ms B: 10
In Ms C: 9
In the Letters: 25
In the Poems: 12
In the Plays (Recreations): 7
In the Yellow Notebook (*Last Conversations*): 7
For a more detailed work, one can refer to the *New Centenary Edition* (Cerf-DDB, 1992):
— *Autobiographical Manuscripts*: p. 441.
— *General Correspondence*, vol. II: p. 1351.
— *Pious Recreations*: p. 473.
— *Last Conversations*: pp. 853-854. Cf. Index, p. 902.

It is understood that a thorough work must not be satisfied with identifying explicit quotations. It is necessary to identify the occurrence of *words, images, symbols* and *turns of phrase*; nor must we forget the biblical quotations that Thérèse had found in St. John of the Cross,[1] and there are also unconscious memories. Concerning this last source, we find in André Bord's *Jean de la Croix en France*, pp. 204, 209, some interesting examples. I restrict myself here to one of them:

Thérèse spoke about the "arms of Jesus" as an "elevator" lifting her to holiness. For this to happen, she had to abandon herself like a child (Ms C, p. 208 [3r°]).

On his part, John of the Cross wrote: "The soul thereby imitates children and their mothers carrying them in their arms so as to spare them the trouble of walking. (...) The soul advances more rapidly than if she walked herself, also when she doesn't feel it, because God carries her in his arms, (...) the soul then has only one thing to do. This is to remain in the hands of God and to abandon herself to her father's conduct with total confidence" (F 3, 3; Œ/J, p. 1163).[2]

Is there a direct influence here? I don't know. It's quite probable; there is a parallel between the thoughts.

II. The Bristol bookmark in the infirmary

In the copy of the *Spiritual Canticle* and *The Living Flame of Love* combined in one volume, an index card of 14 x 3.3 cm. (5½ x 1½ in. approx.) was found with the lower-right corner torn. With her little pencil — which she used for writing the last pages of her final manuscript — she had written down page numbers in a shaky handwriting.

This gives proof that despite her great sufferings and her weakness, the dying Thérèse was still reading her favorite writings.

---

[1] "Of the 168 references to Holy Scripture in the *Story of a Soul*, 48 are likewise found in John, certainly five times, seven times, as many as nine times" (A. Bord, *op. cit.*, p. 208).

[2] [This quotation can't be found in K-RJ — Trans.]

One reads on this bookmark, from top to bottom:

on the front: p. 331 3rd line   *on the back*:
             p. 332 the last   p.p. F Var (? unreadable)
             __3
             p. 335 life
             337-387 s-
             339
             Proverbs 8, v. 31
             274 She has   Without doubt, to arrive
             276 4th li   to this delicious de(ath)
             282-320   one must

Here is the sense the *Last Conversations*, pp. 493-494, makes out of it:

P. 331, 3rd line. Commentary on stanza 23 of the *Spiritual Canticle*, which begins thus: "[the Bridegroom reveals his wonderful secrets to the soul…] with remarkable ease and frequency, for true and perfect love knows not how to keep anything hidden from the beloved, etc." [K-RJ, p. 563].

P. 332, the la(st lines). Commentary on the same stanza:
       "On the tree of the cross [human nature] was redeemed and restored when he gave it there, [through] his passion and death, the hand of his favor and mercy, and broke down the barriers between God and humans that were built up through original sin" [*idem.*].

P. 333. Commentary on some verses from stanza 23:
       "Beneath the apple tree,
       there I took you for my own,
       there I offered you my hand" [*idem.*]

P. 335 life. Thérèse had circled this reference on the bookmark. It concerns the quotation that John of the Cross made of Ezekiel 16:5-14. Thérèse had quoted this passage in her Ms A, pp. 101-102 (47rº), [K-RJ, pp. 564-565].

Pp. 337-338. P. 339. Commentary on stanza 24 and the beginning of the commentary on the verse, "Our bed is in flower" [K-RJ, p. 565].

Proverbs 8:31. The quotation "My delights are with the children of the earth" is found on [K-RJ] p. 566.

P. 274 She has. Commentary on stanza 17 of the *Spiritual Canticle*:
"…her entire aim is to please her Bridegroom.
'Be still, deadening north wind'" [K-RJ, p. 543].
What follows is the commentary on this verse, applied to spiritual dryness.

P. 276 4th li(ne). After the commentary on the verse: "breathe through my garden." The 4th line begins: "It should be noted that the bride does not say 'breathe into my garden,' etc." [K-RJ, p. 543].

P. 282-320. End of the commentary on sta. 17, then the commentary on stanzas 18-23, up to their "Explanation," exclusive.

It would be interesting to pursue this study, for it would expand and deepen our previous remarks. But this final reading of these two major works of St. John of the Cross shows that *Thérèse, sick and dying, was rereading her life in the light of the teachings of St. John of the Cross.*

III. Some opinions about the influence of St. John of the Cross on St. Thérèse of Lisieux.

"St. John of the Cross certainly helped me to understand our Saint."

Mother Isabelle of the Sacred Heart.
(Subprioress of the Carmel of Lisieux, died in 1914 at the age of 32.)

"Now I can no longer read St. John of the Cross without connecting his doctrine to our little St. Thérèse. I find unfathomable depths in these connections that are so just…. Only, St. John of the

Cross shows us the naked cross and Thérèse the cross covered with flowers, but thorns, to be unlike St. John, don't exist at all...."

Fr. Travert.
(Chaplain of the Carmel of Lisieux from 1923 to 1942.
Said to Sr. Marie of the Trinity in 1942.)

"The Church presents to us these Bachelor-of-mystical-science guides, doctors of the science of love. They are St. Teresa of Avila, the spiritual mother (now a Doctor of the Church since 1970); St. John of the Cross, the mystical Doctor; St. Thérèse of the Child Jesus, their daughter, the greatest teacher of spiritual life in modern times, one of the greatest of all times."

Fr. Marie-Eugène of the Child Jesus, O.C.D.
(Je veux voir Dieu, pp. 320–21.)

"It was contact with St. John of the Cross that supplied the personal genius of St. Thérèse of Lisieux with the occasion to spread her own wings. Likewise inspired by him, in the manner of great artistic creators, she became herself, keeping her limpid childlike gaze upon everything."

Fr. Philipon, O.P.
(St. Thérèse de Lisieux, DDB, 1946, p. 31.)

"In her originality and her total independence of expression, St. Thérèse of the Child Jesus is closer to St. John of the Cross than are certain literary commentators, certain amateur readers of *The Ascent of Mount Carmel*. Imitation is always inauthentic but it is even more dangerous in the mystical realm."

Fr. Lucien de St.-Marie, O.C.D.
(Actualité de saint Jean de la Croix, Cerf, 1968, p. 12.)

"Without a title, Thérèse has become a veritable Doctor of the Church, as much as her spiritual Father (John of the Cross) from whom she received so much encouragement. (But) she has kept her originality."

Fr. Conrad De Meester, O.C.D.

(AL, May 1991, num. 701, p. 3.)

"Thérèse will be the Doctor of mystical awakening for the 21st century."

Br. Ephraïm.

(Sur Marthe Robin, published by Lion of Juda, 1990, p. 90.)

"Thérèse received from John a language, a style of life, a doctrine, a double portion of his spirit (Ms B, p. 195 [4r°]), which testifies to being a perfect spiritual daughter. Thérèse is going to transmit to the general public of our era the essential message of John of the Cross and its exigency which is that of Love."

André Bord.

(Jean de la Croix en France, p. 218.)

"From its first form, Thérèse's vocation is a vocation of 'compassion' in the most precise sense: for and with sinners. It is thus that Christ, making himself one with sinners in the darkness of their same sin, saved them by continuing to love them divinely, combined with a desolation more pressing than anything any one of them could ever know. To thus associate herself with Christ even to the extreme of his 'My God, my God, why have you forsaken me?' — this is truly to participate in redemption by sharing in the love which is its soul, in its wholeness. Notwithstanding, it is to plunge without hesitation into a night more profound than even the dark night of faith that John of the Cross spoke about. (…) If the word 'co-redemption' can have a meaning, it is only if there exists for the Christian such a possibility of uniting oneself to Christ in some way while here on earth."

Fr. Louis Bouyer.

(Figures mystiques féminines, Thérèse de Lisieux, pp. 134-135.)

BIBLIOGRAPHY

I. Works of St. Thérèse of Lisieux

1. French titles by Thérèse of the Child Jesus or about her, that have been translated into English:

* *Story of a Soul: The Autobiography of St. Thérèse of Lisieux*, translated from the original manuscript by John Clarke, OCD (Washington, DC: ICS Publications, 1996) (3rd edition), pp. 9-182; authorized translation of *Histoire d'une âme* (Paris: Editions du Cerf-Desclée de Brouwer, 1972).

    — Ms A: Autobiographical manuscript of Thérèse, written for Mother Agnès of Jesus, 1895 (*Story of a Soul*, pp. 13-182).

    — Ms B: Autobiographical manuscript of Thérèse, written for Sr. Marie of the Sacred Heart, Sept. 1896 (*Story of a Soul*, pp. 183-200).

    — Ms C: Autobiographical manuscript of Thérèse, written for Mother Marie de Gonzague, June-July 1897 (*Story of a Soul*, pp. 201-259).

* CJ: The "Yellow Notebook" of her sister Pauline (Mother Agnès of Jesus), *St. Thérèse of Lisieux: Her Last Conversations*, translated from the original manuscripts by John Clarke, OCD (Washington, DC: ICS Publications, Institute of Carmelite Studies, 1977), pp. 35-207; authorized translation of *J'entre dans la vie*, Derniers Entretiens[1] (Paris: Editions du Cerf-Desclée de Brouwer, 1973).

---

[1] Concerning the historical and spiritual value of *Derniers Entretiens* (sayings of the sick Thérèse gathered by Mother Agnès of Jesus and her sisters [contained in *Her Last Conversations*]), cf. my introduction to *Derniers Entretiens*, NEC, Cerf-DDB, 1992, pp. 21-146. [See also the author's comments in *St. Thérèse of Lisieux: Her Life, Times, and Teaching*. Conrad De Meester, gen. ed. (Washington, DC: ICS Publications, 1997), p. 239.] For a critical study of each saying, refer back to the synopsis of the four versions of Mother Agnès of Jesus, called "Last Words" (*Derniers Paroles*, NEC, 1992, p. 504).

- DE: Last Conversations with her sister Céline (Sr. Geneviève), *St. Thérèse of Lisieux: Her Last Conversations*, translated from the original manuscripts by John Clarke, OCD (Washington, DC: ICS Publications, Institute of Carmelite Studies, 1977), pp. 214-230; authorized translation of *J'entre dans la vie, Derniers Entretiens* (Paris: Editions du Cerf-Desclée de Brouwer, 1973).

- *Letters of St. Thérèse of Lisieux, General Correspondence*, 2 volumes (GC I and GC II), translated from the original manuscripts by John Clarke, OCD (Washington, DC: ICS Publications, Institute of Carmelite Studies, Centenary Edition 1973); authorized translation of *Correspondance générale de Thérèse* (Paris: Editions du Cerf-Desclée de Brouwer, 1974; 2 volumes: CG I and CG II).

- *The Poetry of St. Thérèse of Lisieux*, translated by Donald Kinny, OCD (Washington, DC: ICS Publications, Institute of Carmelite Studies, 1996); authorized translation of *Poésies de Thérèse* (Paris: Editions du Cerf-Desclée de Brouwer, 1979).

- *The Prayers of Saint Thérèse of Lisieux*, translated by Aletheia Kane, OCD (Washington, DC: ICS Publications, Institute of Carmelite Studies, 1997); authorized translation of *Prières de Thérèse* (Paris: Editions du Cerf-Desclée de Brouwer, 1988).

2. French titles

- *Nouvelle Édition du Centenaire* [New Centenary Edition], Editions du Cerf-Desclée de Brouwer, 1992, comprising eight volumes:

  a. *Manuscrits autobiographiques* [Autobiographical Manuscripts]
  - Manuscript A (1895) addressed to Mother Agnès of Jesus
  - Manuscript B (September 1896) addressed to Sr. Marie of the Sacred Heart
  - Manuscript C (June-July 1897) addressed to Mother Marie de Gonzague

  b. *Correspondance générale (2 volumes)* [General Correspondence] 266 Letters of Thérèse and those of her correspondents

  c. *Poésies* [Poems] 54 Poems (1893-1897)

d. *Théâtre* [Theater]
   8 Recreations (1893-1897)

e. *Prières* [Prayers]
   21 Prayers

f. *Derniers Entretiens* [Last Conversations]
   Last sayings gathered by her sisters during her final illness (2 volumes)

   This edition also exists as a single volume, *Œuvres complètes* [Complete Works], Editions du Cerf-Desclée de Brouwer, 1992, 1600 pages: the entire texts with introductions and fewer notes.

- *La Bible avec Thérèse de Lisieux* (Paris: Editions du Cerf-Desclée de Brouwer, 1995). (*The Bible with Thérèse of Lisieux.*)
- RP: *Recréations pieuses de Thérèse* [Plays], *numerotées* (Théâtre au Carmel, Editions du Cerf-Desclée de Brouwer, 1985).
- Revue *Annales de Lisieux* [Magazine *Annals of Lisieux*].

2. Testimonies and various documents about St. Thérèse of Lisieux

- *Carnet Rouge*, rédigé par sœur Marie de la Trinité, published in VT 74 and 75. [*Red Notebook*, edited by Sr. Marie of the Trinity.]
- *Conseils et Souvenirs*, rédigé par sœur Marie de la Trinité, published in VT 73 and 77. [*Counsels and Reminiscences*, edited by Sr. Marie of the Trinity.]
- *Notes des Carmelites préparatoires au Procès apostolique de Thérèse.* [Preparatory notes of the Carmelites for the Apostolic Process.]
- *Procès de l'ordinaire* [Bishop's Process], Rome 1973.
- *Procès apostolique* [Apostolic Process], Rome, 1976.
- Magazine *Vie thérésienne* [Thérésian Life], 14100 Lisieux, 31, rue du Carmel
  — Especially VT 73, 74, 75, 77 (Notebooks of Sr. Marie of the Trinity)
  — *Le carnet scripturaire de Thérèse* [Thérèse's biblical notebook]:

- VT 78 (April 1980), pp. 146-160
- VT 79 (July 1980), pp. 215-240
- VT 80 (January 1981), pp. 60-68
  (All these articles signed D.C.L. are by Sr. Cécile, OCD.)

P. DESCOUVEMONT AND H.N. LOOSE, *Thérèse et Lisieux* [Thérèse and Lisieux], Cerf, OAA, OCL, Novalis, 1991, pp. 170-173.

_____, *Sainte Thérèse de Lisieux, La vie en images* [St. Thérèse of Lisieux, her life in pictures], Cerf, OAA, OCL, Novalis, 1995. On John of the Cross, pp. 350-353.

SR. GENEVIÈVE, *Conseils et Souvenirs* [Counsels and Reminiscences], Foi Vivante, Cerf, 1988. Especially pp. 51, 70, 80, 148, 160, 162, 192. Authorized translation by the Carmelite Nuns of New York under the title *A Memoir of My Sister, St. Thérèse* (New York: P. J. Kenedy & Sons, 1959).

Visage de Thérèse de Lisieux (Lisieux: OCL, 2 volumes, 1961), in two volumes with numbered photos of Thérèse. Translated by Peter-Thomas Rohrbach, under the title *The Photo Album of St. Thérèse of Lisieux* (New York: P. J. Kenedy & Sons, 1962).

II. Works of St. John of the Cross

1. Used by Thérèse

- The *Cantique spirituel et Le Vive Flamme d'Amour* [The Spiritual Canticle and the Living Flame of Love], translated by the Carmelites of Paris, Douniol et Cie, ed., 1875, in a single volume (precise description in DE, p. 843). XIV + 416 + 379 pages.

  At the end there are two sermons preached by Msgr. Landriot, archbishop of Reims, to the Carmelites of Reims on November 24, 1867 and November 24, 1872, pp. 315-366. They can be read in VT 144 and 145 with an introduction and notes by Sr. Cécile, OCD (we usually quote this edition, which was Thérèse's).

- *Maximes et Avis spirituels de notre Bienheureux Père Jean de la Crois*

[Maxims and Spiritual Advice of our Blessed Father John of the Cross], translated by the Carmelites of Paris, published by H. Oudin, 1895, 106 pages. *It is an anthology drawn from the Saint's works. It is therefore impossible to refer to the usual editions* [emphasis — Trans.]

2. *Œuevres complètes [Complete Works] of St. John of the Cross, Cerf, 1990, 1 volume, 1872 pages. Translation by Mother Marie of the Blessed Sacrament, OCD. Edition organized, revised and presented by Dominique Poirot, OCD.*

Because the reader doesn't have available the texts read by Thérèse, we refer to this edition in parentheses (ŒJ).

3. *Titles of the works of St. John of the Cross that have been translated into English:*

• *The Collected Works of St. John of the Cross*, rev. ed., translated by Kieran Kavanaugh, OCD, and Otilio Rodriguez, OCD, ICS Publications, Institute of Carmelite Studies, Washington, DC, 1991.
   — *The Ascent of Mount Carmel*, pp. 113-349.
   — *The Living Flame of Love*, pp. 638-715.
   — *The Dark Night*, pp. 358-457.
   — *The Spiritual Canticle*; Thérèse read the B version given here, pp. 469-630. Where this translation differs from the French text cited by the author, CSB will indicate the copy that Thérèse used.

III. Various

Crisogono de Jésus Sacramentado, *Vida de San Juan de la cruz* [Life of St. John of the Cross], (Biblioteca de autores cristianos, 435), Madrid, le editorial Católica, 11th ed. 1982. French translation of the 1974 edition by Pierre Serouet, ocd, *Jean de la Croix. Sa vie*, Cerf, 1982, 404 pages.

P. Marie-Eugène de l'enfant-Jésus
   — *Je veux voir Dieu* [I want to see God], Carmel, ed., 1949,

especially, pp. 821-859. See the analytical table, Doctrine: p. 1091.

— *Jean de la Croix. Présence de lumière* [John of the Cross, Presence of light], Carmel, ed., 1991.

— *Triduum* [Three days] on St. Thérèse of Lisieux, at Lisieux, 1927.

— *Retraite sacerdotale* [Priestly retreat] at Notre-Dame de Vie, September 1965, extracts found in *Ton amour grandi avec moi. Un génie spirituel, Thérèse de Lisieux* [Your love has grown with me. A spiritual genius, Thérèse of Lisieux], Carmel, ed., 1987, pp. 31-80. Published in English as *Under the Torrent of His Love: Thérèse of Lisieux, a Spiritual Genius*, New York: Alba House, 1995.

— "Sainte Thérèse de l'Enfant-Jésus, docteur de la vie mystique" [St. Thérèse of the Child Jesus, doctor of mystical life], Institut catholique de Paris, 1947, in *Ton amour a grandi avec moi*, pp. 85-169; (*Under the Torrent of His Love*, pp. 65-155).

A. Combes, *Introduction à la spiritualité de sainte Thérèse de l'Enfant-Jésus* [Introduction to the spirituality of St. Thérèse of the Child Jesus], Vrin, 1948.

A. Bord, *Jean de la Croix en France* [John of the Cross in France], Beauchesne, 1993. On Thérèse of Lisieux, pp. 203-218.

Angel de les Gavarres, *Carisma de Terese de Lisieux. Su itinerario espiritual a la luz de sus Manuscritos autobiograficos* [The charism of Thérèse of Lisieux. Her spiritual journey in light of her autobiographical manuscripts], Barcelona, Esinsa, 1993, 364 pages (I haven't read this book which matches the thérésian journey to sanjuanist stages).

Conrad de Meester, *Dynamique de la confiance: Genèse et structure de la "voie d'enfance spirituelle" de saint Thérèse de Lisieux*, Paris: Cerf, 1995; *The Power of Confidence: Genesis and Structure of the "Way of Spiritual Childhood" of St. Thérèse of Lisieux*, New York: Alba House, 1998.

P. Descouvemont, *Une novice de Sainte Thérèse: Soeur Marie de la Trinité*, Paris: Cerf, 1993; *Thérèse of Lisieux and Marie of the Trinity*, New York: Alba House, 1997.

FREDERICK L. MILLER, *The Trial of Faith of St. Thérèse of Lisieux*, New York: Alba House, 1998.

FRANÇOIS JAMART, OCD, *The Complete Spiritual Doctrine of St. Thérèse of Lisieux*, New York: Alba House, 1961 (13th Printing, 1997).

IV. Articles concerning the influence of St. John of the Cross on St. Thérèse of the Child Jesus and of the Holy Face (in chronological order)

CLAUDIO DE JÉSUS CRUCIFICADO, OCD, "La Beata Teresa del Niño Jesús, discipula fiel de san Juan de la Cruz" [Blessed Thérèse of the Child Jesus, faithful disciple of St. John of the Cross], *El Monte Carmelo*, num. 27, 1923, pp. 285-291, 464-467, 530-534.

BRUNO DE JÉSUS-MARIE, OCD, "La Fille de saint Jean de la Croix" [Daughter of St. John of the Cross], *Carmel* 10, 5/18/1925, pp. 136-142.

PAUL TRAVERT, "Saint Jean de la Croix et sainte Thérèse de l'Enfant-Jésus" [St. John of the Cross and St. Thérèse of the Child Jesus], *Annales de Lisieux*, 1927, pp. 161-164.

LUCIEN-MARIE DE SAINT-JOSEPH, OCD, "Renouveau thérésien" [Thérèsian renewal], *Études carmélitaines*, vol. II, October 1935. On Thérèse of Lisieux, pp. 133-144.

LOUIS DE LA TRINITÉ, OCD, "Sainte Thérèse de Lisieux dans la spiritualité du Carmel" [St. Thérèse of Lisieux in the spirituality of Carmel], *Études et Documents*, 8, 1939, pp. 64-78.

PIERRE BLANCHARD, "Sainte Thérèse de l'Enfant-Jésus, fille de saint Jean de la Croix" [St. Thérèse of the Child Jesus, daughter of St. John of the Cross], *L'Année théologique*, 8, 1947, pp. 425-438.

P. MARIE-EUGÈNE DE L'ENFANT-JÉSUS, OCD, "La Doctrine de Saint Jean de la Croix," *Sainte Thérèse de l'Enfant-Jésus, docteur de la vie mystique* [The doctrine of St. John of the Cross *in* St. Thérèse of the Child Jesus, doctor of mystical life], Carmel, Petit Castelet - Tarascon, Sept.-Oct. 1947, pp. 150-153.

GABRIEL DE SAINTE MARIE-MADELEINE, OCD, "Thérèse et Jean de la

Croix" [Thérèse and John of the Cross], preface to
l'Introduction à la spiritualité de Thérèse de l'Enfant-Jésus
[Introduction to the spirituality of Thérèse of the Child Jesus],
by André Combes, appeared in Italian, Firenze, 1949.

LUCIEN DE SAINTE-MARIE, OCD, "Thérèse de Lisieux ou l'enfance unie
à la maturité" [Thérèse of Lisieux or childhood united with
maturity], *La Vie spirituelle*, vol. 85, 1952, pp. 304-323.

STANISLAS FUMET, *Mikaël. Qui est comme Dieu?* [Michael, Who is like
God?] Cerf, 1954, 246 pages. On Thérèse, pp. 165-215.

CH. A. BERNARD, "L'Influence de saint Jean de la Croix sur sainte
Thérèse de l'Enfant-Jésus" [The influence of St. John of the
Cross on St. Thérèse of the Child Jesus], *Revue d'ascetique et
de mystique*, num. 32, 1956, pp. 69-80.

GENNARO CAMILLO, OCD, "La Fiamma viva e santa Terese del
Bambino Gesu" [The living flame of St. Thérèse of the Child
Jesus], *Rivista di vita spirituale*, 11, 1957, pp. 278-287.

P. GRÉGOIRE DE JÉSUS CRUCIFIÉ, OCD, "Les Nuits sanjuanists vécues par
sainte Thérèse de l'Enfant-Jésus" [Sanjuanist nights experienced by St. Thérèse of the Child Jesus]. Translated from
Spanish, Supplement to *La Vie spirituelle*, no. 63, 1962, pp.
611-643.

P. STÉPHANE-JOSEPH PIAT, "Saint Jean de la Croix et la belle aventure
thérésienne" [St. John of the Cross and the beautiful thérèsian
adventure], *Vie thérésienne*, num. 19, 1965, pp. 141-152.

M.-D. POINSENET, "Voie d'enfance spirituelle de Montée du Carmel,
Thérèse de Lisieux et Jean de la Croix" [The way of spiritual
childhood of the Ascent of Carmel, Thérèse of Lisieux and
John of the Cross], *Vie thérésienne*, num. 17, 1965, pp. 11-24.

MARIACHER MARIA-NOEMI, *Una spiritualita viva: S. Giovanni delle
Cruce e Santa teresa di Lisieux* [A living spirituality: St. John of
the Cross and St. Thérèse of Lisieux], Roma, Centro Studi
USMI, 1973, 112 pages.

SIMEON DE LA SAGRADA FAMILIA, OCD, "Presencia de S. Juan de la Cruz
en la vida y en los escritos de santa Teresa del Niño Jesús"
[Presence of St. John of the Cross in the life and writings of
St. Thérèse of the Child Jesus], *El Monte Carmelo*, no. 81,

1973, pp. 333-358; no. 82, 1974, pp. 365-378; no. 83, 1975, pp. 319-329.

CHRISTOPHER LATIMER, "Thérèse and the Dark Night," *Little Flower* 55, 1975, no. 5, pp. 19-23; no. 6, pp. 16-22.

SENTIEN EMETERIO GARCIA, OCD, "Monte Carmelo y santa Teresita del Niño Jesús" [Mount Carmel and St. Thérèse of the Child Jesus], *El Monte Carmelo*, no. 83, 1975 pp. 93-136.

ERNEST MURA, "Thérèse à l'école du Docteur mystique" [Thérèse at the school of the mystical Doctor], *Vie thérésienne*, 1977, no. 66, pp. 108-118.

FRANÇOIS GIRARD, "Dans le Christ total: de Jean de la Croix à Thérèse de l'Enfant-Jésus," *Jésus-Christ, rédempteur de l'homme* [In the Whole Christ of John of the Cross and Thérèse of the Child Jesus *in* Jesus Christ, redeemer of the world], Carmel, 1986, pp. 227-260.

MICHEL GRISON, "Thérèse de Lisieux, disciple de saint Jean de la Croix", *Thérèse de Lisieux parmi ses frères les saints* [Thérèse of Lisieux, disciple of St. John of the Cross *in* Thérèse of Lisieux among her brothers the saints], Saint Paul, 1987, pp. 119-136.

EMMANUEL RENAULT, "Presence de saint Jean de la Croix dans la vie et les écrits de sainte Thérèse de l'Enfant-Jésus" [Presence of St. John of the Cross in the life and writings of St. Thérèse of the Child Jesus], *Carmel*, 1990/3, no. 58, pp. 2-30. Reprinted in *Vie thérésienne*, no. 121, 1991, pp. 29-51.

MARGARET DORGAN, OCD, "Thérèse, a Later-Day Interpreter of John of the Cross," *Experiencing St. Thérèse Today*, ICS Publications, Washington, 1990, pp. 97-118.

CONRAD DE MEESTER, *in Dutch*:
1. "De orkestleider en de violiste" [The conductor and the violinist], *Innerlijk Leven*, 45, 1991, pp. 6-20.
2. "Als de leerlinge er (haast) evenveel van weet..." [When the disciple knows (almost) as much], *ibid.*, pp. 138-152.
3. "Groeien naar volmaakte twee-ééheid" [To grow towards perfect unity], *ibid.*, pp. 224-239.
4. "Het strijkstokprobleem van Thérèse van Lisieux" [The outstanding problem of Thérèse of Lisieux], *ibid.*, pp. 280-291.

5. "Twee door God gefascineerde leraars" [Two Doctors fasci-
nated by God], *ibid.*, pp. 340-356.

GABRIELE DI S.M. MADDALENA, OCD, "Nella luce di san Giovanni della
Croce" [In the light of St. John of the Cross], *Santa Teresa di
Lisieux,* Carmelo S. Giuseppe, Roma, 1991. Repeat of
previous articles, "S. Giovanni della Croce maestro e padre di
S. Teresa de Gesu Bambino" [St. John of the Cross, master
and father of St. Thérèse of the Child Jesus], pp. 47-75.

GUY GAUCHER, "Mourir d'amour dans *La Vive Flamme,*" in *Jean de la
Croix, un saint, un maître* ["To die of love in The Living
Flame," *in* John of the Cross, a saint, a master], Carmel, ed.
1992, pp. 315-351.